A HISTORY OF THE EASTER RISING IN 50 OBJECTS

JOHN GIBNEY

FOUNDED IN 1828
GLASNEVIN TRUST
DARDISTOWN GLASNEVIN GOLDENBRIDGE
NEWLANDS CROSS PALMERSTOWN

MERCIER PRESS
IRISH PUBLISHER – IRISH STORY

MERCIER PRESS

Cork

www.mercierpress.ie

© John Gibney, 2016

ISBN: 978 1 78117 381 7

10 9 8 7 6 5 4 3 2 1

A CIP record for this title is available from the British Library

This book is sold subject to the condition that it shall not, by way of trade or otherwise, be lent, resold, hired out or otherwise circulated without the publisher's prior consent in any form of binding or cover other than that in which it is published and without a similar condition including this condition being imposed on the subsequent purchaser.

No part of this publication may be reproduced or transmitted in any form or by any means, electronic or mechanical, including photocopying, recording or any information or retrieval system, without the prior permission of the publisher in writing.

Printed and bound in the EU.

Contents

Acknowledgements 6
Introduction 7

01 Tom Clarke's Certificate of US Naturalisation, 1905
Reviving Republicanism 11

02 Abbey Theatre Programme for a Play by
Thomas MacDonagh, 1908
Cultural Nationalism 16

03 Seán MacDiarmada's Hurley
From GAA to IRB 20

04 *An Scoláire*: St Enda's Student Magazine
A School for Revolution 24

05 A Bill from St Enda's to Éamonn Ceannt
Reviving a Language 28

06 The Ulster Covenant, 1912
Ulster Unionism and Resistance to Home Rule 31

07 Irish Citizen Army Flag
Class Conflict in the Irish Revolution 35

08 Diarmuid Lynch's Irish Volunteer Uniform
The Militarisation of Irish Nationalism 40

09 Cumann na mBan Brooch
Irish Women and Irish Revolution 44

10 A Baton used in the Howth Gun-running
Raising the Stakes 48

11 Irish National Volunteers Uniform
The Great War and the Volunteer Split 52

12 Manuscript of Patrick Pearse's Oration at the
Funeral of Jeremiah O'Donovan Rossa, 1915
A Statement of Intent 56

13 Uniform for Roger Casement's 'Irish Brigade'
Gallant Allies in Europe 60

14 Mosin-Nagant Rifle from the *Aud*
A Crucial Failure 64

15 Teacups used by the Pearse Brothers
Calm before the Storm 69

16	Mobilisation Order for 'B' Company, 1st Battalion, Dublin Brigade, Irish Volunteers, 24 April 1916	
	The Rising Begins	73
17	A Poster for the Coliseum Theatre, 24 April 1916	
	A Day Like Any Other	78
18	Proclamation of the Irish Republic	
	The Manifesto	83
19	Irish Republic Flag	
	The Occupation of the GPO	88
20	*Irish War News*	
	The First Days of the Rising	93
21	Homemade Bomb	
	Desperate Measures	97
22	A Cricket Bat that Died for Ireland	
	Looting and Street-fighting	101
23	Memorial Cup awarded for the Defence of Trinity College, Dublin	
	A Loyal Garrison	104
24	Wesley Hanna's Account of the Rising	
	A Civilian Perspective	110
25	Watercolour Sketch of a Barricade at the Shelbourne Hotel	
	The British Response	114
26	Certificate of Service for the 16th (Irish) Division, 27 April 1916	
	The Easter Rising and the Great War	119
27	Compensation Claim for Damage to 73 and 73a Lower Mount Street	
	The Ambush at Mount Street Bridge	123
28	Fianna Hat belonging to Seán Healy	
	Death of a Boy Soldier	127
29	Royal Irish Constabulary Carbine from the Battle of Ashbourne	
	The Rising in Meath and Co. Dublin	130
30	A Globe belonging to Liam Mellows	
	The Rising in East Galway	134
31	James Connolly's Blood-stained Shirt	
	A Wounded Visionary	138
32	Artefacts from the *Helga*	
	A Mistaken Impression	142
33	Rubble and Cartridges from the GPO	
	A Souvenir of Sackville Street	146

34	Handkerchief embroidered in Marrowbone Lane, 30 April 1916	
	The Fighting in South-west Dublin	150
35	A Fragment of a Wall from 16 Moore Street inscribed by Thomas Clarke	
	Surrender	154
36	A Book damaged by Gunfire from Marsh's Library	
	Collateral Damage	158
37	Dublin Fire Brigade Helmet	
	The Destruction of Dublin	161
38	*The Evening Sun*, 1 May 1916	
	Reporting the Rising	165
39	Burial Register for Prospect Cemetery, General Grounds	
	Victims	168
40	British Public Notice, 11 May 1916	
	Repression	171
41	Playing Cards used by Thomas MacDonagh in Captivity	
	The Executions	175
42	Thomas Kent's Rosary Beads	
	The Rising in Cork	179
43	Platter used by Sir Roger Casement during his Appeal against his Conviction for Treason, July 1916	
	The Execution of Sir Roger Casement	183
44	Biscuits given to Kathleen Lynn in Prison	
	Captivity	187
45	Wood Carving made by a Prisoner in Frongoch	
	Frongoch and the Prison Experience	191
46	1916 Memorial Card bought in 17 Moore Street, 1917	
	Changing Opinions on the Rising	196
47	Handcuffs used on Thomas Ashe, 1917	
	Republicans after the Rising	200
48	Letter from Michael Collins to Patrick Fogarty giving Notice of Compensation for Imprisonment, 1917	
	From Easter Rising to War of Independence	204
49	'Up De Valera', 'Up Griffith': Sinn Féin Badges from the 1918 General Election	
	The Victory of Sinn Féin, 1918	208
50	Sigerson Monument, Glasnevin Cemetery	
	The Contested Legacies of the Rising	212
Picture Credits for Main Images		217
Select Bibliography		219
Index		222

Acknowledgements

I would like to thank the following people for offering suggestions and for helping to obtain and understand the material used in this book: Julie Burke (Marsh's Library); Lorcan Collins; Mairéad Delaney (Abbey Theatre); Conor Dodd (Glasnevin Trust); Las Fallon; Brian Hanley; Michael Hanna; Sandra Heise (National Museum of Ireland); Brian Hughes (Letters of 1916 project); Lar Joye (National Museum of Ireland); Rosemary King (Allen Library); Sinead McCoole (Jackie Clarke Collection); Brian Ó Conchubair; Seán Seosamh Ó Conchubair; Susan Schreibmann (Letters of 1916 project); and Aoife Torpey (Kilmainham Gaol Museum). Thanks are also due to Mary Feehan and all at Mercier Press, and to the staff of the Tyrone Guthrie Centre at Annaghmakerrig, Co. Monaghan. Finally, profound thanks to Liza Costello for her patience, love and support. Any errors and omissions are, of course, my own.

Introduction

On 24 April 1916 – Easter Monday – groups of separatist republicans seized a number of buildings around Dublin, most notably the General Post Office (GPO) on the main thoroughfare of Sackville Street (later O'Connell Street). A manifesto proclaiming the existence of an Irish Republic as a 'sovereign independent state' was read aloud outside the building and posted up around the city. Over the next five days perhaps as many as 20,000 British troops, many of whom were of Irish birth, occupied Dublin and much of the city centre was devastated.

The Easter Rising of 1916 took place during the First World War and would not have happened when it did had the war not been ongoing. Members of the secretive Irish Republican Brotherhood (IRB) planned the rebellion, and a number of small paramilitary organisations took part in it. That being said, the Rising that broke out was not the Rising that seems to have been planned. There had been an unsuccessful attempt to import weapons from Germany before the rebellion, and this failure ensured that, at the eleventh hour, attempts were made to call off a rebellion that was surely robbed of any prospect of success. The Rising that *did* break out was mainly a Dublin affair and perhaps as few as 2,500 rebels, both men and women, took part in it. Although there were some ambushes and skirmishes in the counties of Meath and Galway, some republicans assembled in Cork city and others seized the town of Enniscorthy in Co. Wexford, the bulk of the fighting was in Dublin and the British authorities took the events there very seriously indeed, not least because of their suspicions that Germany might be involved. The rebel Proclamation, after all, spoke of the assistance provided by 'gallant allies in Europe'. Hence the massive mobilisation of troops to crush the insurrection, both from within Ireland and from Britain; indeed, events happened so rapidly that some soldiers disembarking from ships in Dublin supposedly thought that they were in France. Martial law was declared on Tuesday 25 April, and from Thursday the rebel positions were being bombarded by artillery. By the time that the insurgent forces surrendered on 29 April, over 360 people had been killed, approximately 2,600 had been wounded, and much of Dublin's city centre had been laid waste. After less than a week, the rebellion was over.

So what is so special about the Easter Rising? Admittedly, the spectacular destruction of much of central Dublin was without precedent and marked the moment when the Great War finally came to Irish shores (many contemporaries reached for the language of the war to make sense of what had happened). Yet any onlooker standing in the ruins of the city in May 1916 was bearing witness to the aftermath of a rebellion that had been crushed. However, timing is everything and many contemporary observers perceptively realised that what had happened in Dublin over Easter Week would have an impact above and beyond the event itself. Coming when it did, and as it did, the Easter Rising and its aftermath became the catalyst for the independence movement that arose in Ireland in the years that followed.

The Rising came as a complete surprise to most of the Irish people and to the British administration. There had been no serious separatist uprising in Ireland since the failed Fenian rebellion of 1867 (presumably one of those referred to in the Proclamation), and in the forty-nine years between 1867 and 1916 Ireland had changed enormously. Politically, the brief window opened for separatism in the 1860s had closed as it came to be overshadowed by the cause of Irish 'Home Rule' – the demand for a devolved government in Dublin – that had emerged from the 1870s onwards, and the parallel emergence of Irish unionism.

However, a revival of republican separatism around the turn of the twentieth century dovetailed with a renewed interest in the revival of Irish culture in the late Victorian era and the militarisation of Irish politics prompted by the Home Rule crisis of 1912–14. The armed stand-off between nationalist Home Rulers and unionists that emerged after the Liberal government of Herbert Asquith promised to establish a Home Rule parliament for Ireland in the years before the First World War dominated Irish political life in the years before 1916. The Easter Rising came from the margins, but the significance of the Rising is that it brought the ideology of separatism into Ireland's political mainstream, as one Irish nationalist movement came to be replaced by another in the years after 1916. That is what gives the Easter Rising an enduring relevance.

What this book is intended to do is examine some aspects of the origins, course and outcome of the Rising by exploring the stories attached to a selection of contemporary documents and artefacts that have survived the ravages of time. As a discipline, history naturally prizes the written word, whether in the form of documents that provide empirical evidence, or testimonies that can encapsulate the lived experience of the past. Yet material culture has a story to tell as well; or in this case, stories. Artefacts that now reside in museums and other repositories were seen, touched and used by individuals who witnessed or participated in past events. Such objects are themselves silent witnesses, but their existence can open doors into the past. Some of them may be familiar, some of them may not be, but all of them can reveal aspects of this seminal event in modern Irish history. The Easter Rising might be deemed worthy of either admiration or condemnation, but before one can reach conclusions about the past, one has to look at that past as honestly and as fairly as is possible. The stories that follow constitute a modest attempt to do just that.

01

Tom Clarke's Certificate of US Naturalisation, 1905

Reviving Republicanism

On 2 November 1905 Thomas J. Clarke became a naturalised citizen of the United States of America. His presence there indicates the existence of a republican network straddling the Atlantic Ocean, which was essential to the planning of the Easter Rising.

Republicanism in Ireland can trace its roots back to the United Irishmen of the 1790s and could be defined, at its most basic level, as a tradition of militant separatism demanding complete independence from Britain. In the second half of the nineteenth century the most potent manifestation of republicanism was the IRB (also known as the Fenians), which had been founded in the 1850s. It was a secret oath-bound society dedicated to attaining an independent Irish republic through force of arms. The IRB had staged an unsuccessful rebellion in 1867 and carried out bombing campaigns in British cities in the 1880s, but by the late nineteenth century it had become moribund, and republicanism had become marginalised. 'Physical force' was seen to have failed in its objective of securing Irish independence and, from the 1870s onwards, more modest demands for Irish self-government within the United Kingdom in the form of Home Rule began to emerge. By the 1890s the Home Rule movement essentially held a monopoly on the political allegiance of nationalist Ireland.

Then, around the turn of the twentieth century, smaller and more radical nationalist groupings began to emerge once again. The centenary of the

See Endorsement on back.

No. 7405

UNITED STATES OF AMERICA, } ss.
Southern District of New York,

UNITED STATES OF A

the 2nd day

hundred and five

at present of the City and State of

Citizen of the United Stat

of the United States of America,

passed 14th of April, 1802, and Acts su

"An Act to regulate the immigration of

produced to the Court such evidence and m

and the same having been duly recorded as

admitted, and he was accordingly admitted

In Testimony Whereof, the seal of the said Court is hereunt

our Lord one thousand nine hundred and

Clerk

Examined
O K Drew 1/28/06
Department of Justice.

emembered, That at a **DISTRICT COURT** of the
A, held in and for the Southern District of New York, on
ovember   in the year of our Lord one thousand nine
nas J Clarke

rk, having appeared in said Court and applied to be admitted a
America, pursuant to the directions of the Acts of the Congress
"An Act to establish an uniform rule of Naturalization, etc.,"
passed on that subject, and to the directions of the Act of Congress entitled
the United States," approved March 3, 1903: and having thereupon
eclaration, renunciation and affidavits as are by the said Acts required,
y said Acts, it was **Thereupon Ordered** by the said Court that he be
TIZEN OF THE UNITED STATES OF AMERICA.

this   2nd   day of   Nov   , in the year of
, and of our Independence the one hundred and   thirtieth

rox Alexander

rict Court of the United States for the Southern District of New York, rebellion of the United Irishmen in 1798 gave separatist republicanism a shot in the arm. The revival of more militant nationalism and republicanism, however modest in scale, was also aided by the outbreak of the Boer War, as fringe nationalists expressed solidarity with South African settlers in their struggle against British imperial power. Most importantly, the IRB was discreetly revitalised and quietly repopulated with a new generation of activists – and this brings us back to Thomas J. Clarke.

Thomas Clarke
(*private collection*)

Clarke was born in 1867 on the Isle of Wight; perhaps ironically, given the future trajectory of his life and career, his father, James, was a bombardier in the Royal Artillery. Thomas grew up in Dungannon, Co. Tyrone, and joined the IRB in the late 1870s. He first emigrated to the US in 1880 and joined the IRB's American counterpart, Clan na Gael, but he was arrested in 1883 as he attempted to embark on a bombing campaign in London. Clarke spent the next fifteen years in various British prisons, often in extremely harsh conditions. He was released in 1899 and, while permanently affected by his imprisonment, remained a militant Fenian. Emigrating to the US once again in 1900, he again began to work for Clan na Gael and became close to the veteran Irish republican John Devoy, a relationship that was very significant in later years. He married Kathleen Daly in New York in 1901; she was the niece of John Daly, another veteran Fenian to whom Clarke was close (they had, amongst other things, been imprisoned together at one point). Clarke returned to Ireland in 1907, opened a tobacconist shop in Dublin and became involved in the IRB in earnest once more. He also joined a wide range of 'advanced' nationalist organisations, but his involvement in them was harnessed to a single purpose.

Patrick Pearse and James Connolly are, for many people, the figures who best personify the Easter Rising, yet the Rising could have happened without either of them. The same cannot be said of Clarke. Unlike his more famous colleagues, he chose to work behind the scenes, for both practical and personal reasons – he was no stranger to the authorities and preferred to avoid the limelight – but Clarke was the man who, perhaps more than any other, conceived the Easter Rising. To that end, he sought to manipulate and control militant nationalism in a ruthless, single-minded manner in which virtually all other political, cultural or social programmes were subordinated to the singular purpose of another revolt aimed at ending British rule in Ireland. If any single figure can be said to have been the brains behind the operation, it was Clarke.

Clarke's connections in the United States proved essential to the planning of what became the Easter Rising. In a nod to the Irish-American networks, without whom any attempts to gain material assistance for a rebellion would have come to naught, the eventual manifesto of the Rising – the 'Proclamation' – made reference to 'exiled children in America'. However, the fact of Clarke's US citizenship, as confirmed in the certificate pictured here, did not save him from execution for his own involvement in the Easter Rising.

02

Abbey Theatre Programme for a Play by Thomas MacDonagh, 1908
Cultural Nationalism

The Easter Rising was not a rebellion of poets. Nor was it a rebellion of playwrights. Nevertheless, many of those who fought in it were members of multiple organisations, and some of those who planned it dabbled in literature, to varying degrees of success. One of them was Thomas MacDonagh. This 1908 programme for the Abbey Theatre features a play written by MacDonagh, along with a translation by Lady Augusta Gregory of a comedy by the French playwright Molière. MacDonagh was later executed for his role in the Rising (indeed, he was one of the seven members of the 'military council' responsible for planning it).

Of the myriad groups and organisations that sought to foster a regeneration of Irish cultural, economic and social life in this era, the literary figures associated with the Abbey Theatre, including W. B. Yeats and Lady Gregory, were among the most prominent. The late Victorian cultural revival also threw up a multiplicity of smaller, less well-known theatrical ventures. For many younger nationalists, it was perfectly natural to become involved in cultural activities that had a nationalist complexion, and amateur dramatic productions were certainly amongst these.

MacDonagh was born in Cloughjordan in Co. Tipperary. He initially planned to enter the priesthood, but dropped out and instead became a teacher of English, French and history in Kilkenny and subsequently Cork (both his parents had been National School teachers). He gravitated to 'advanced' nationalism through the Gaelic League (Conradh na Gaeilge) – the most prominent organisation involved in attempts to foster a revival of the Irish language – and spoke Irish fluently, but drifted away from the League after 1905. A cultured and cosmopolitan figure, MacDonagh was by then publishing poetry, and after a stint as a teacher at St Enda's (the boys' school founded by Patrick Pearse), during which he completed a BA at University College, Dublin (UCD), he went on to complete an MA on the Elizabethan poet Thomas Campion. Following this he was appointed a lecturer at the university, a post he held until his death. Politically, he was active in the Irish Volunteers after its foundation in 1913 to counter the threat posed to Home Rule by the formation of the Ulster Volunteer Force in the northern counties, and joined the IRB in 1915. He eventually became involved in the planning of the Rising and, having exhorted his final class in UCD to read the works of Jane Austen, he led the occupation of the Jacob's biscuit factory on Bishop Street until ordered to surrender by Patrick Pearse.

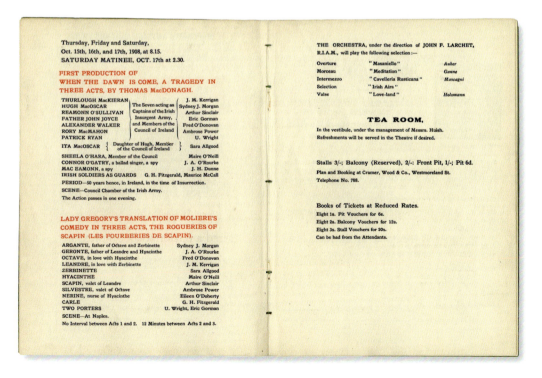

Thomas MacDonagh
(*private collection*)

MacDonagh's literary ventures preceded his political activities. The play showcased here, *When the Dawn is Come*, was originally submitted to the Abbey in 1904. Set fifty years in the future, during a 'time of insurrection' led by a council of seven 'captains of the Irish insurgent army', it tells the story of how one of the generals, Thurlough MacKieran, is falsely accused of being a spy. With the support of the soldiers under his command, he is redeemed by victory on the battlefield, but mortally wounded in the process. MacDonagh described it as 'the story of a young man who has had most to do in getting up the Rising'.[1] W. B. Yeats was intrigued by the play when he first read it and felt MacDonagh had literary potential, but it met with lukewarm reviews. MacDonagh himself was unimpressed with the quality of some of the acting and claimed that the play was misinterpreted, though Yeats had expressed reservations about the dialogue upon reading the early draft. It was the only play MacDonagh produced at the Abbey and it was never performed again, though he continued to revise it in later years.

MacDonagh's involvement with theatre did not end there: in 1914 he became manager of the Irish Theatre Company based on Hardwicke Street in Dublin, which had been founded by Joseph Mary Plunkett (another future 1916 leader) and Edward Martyn. It was intended to provide an alternative forum for Irish plays, as the Abbey was perceived in some quarters to have gone stale. MacDonagh also hosted productions of plays by leading European authors such as Henrik Ibsen.

---

1   Shane Kenna, *16 Lives: Thomas MacDonagh* (Dublin, 2014), p. 55.

The existence of *When the Dawn is Come* illustrates the close and interlocking circles of militant cultural nationalism in the years before the Rising. Years after the Rising, Yeats asked the famous, if self-serving, question, whether or not his play *Cathleen Ní Houlihan* sent out certain men the English shot (such as MacDonagh). The answer has to be no. Yet many younger, 'advanced' nationalists saw artistic expression as vitally important, and the subject matter of the play, with its seven 'generals', has an inevitable echo of what MacDonagh became involved in eight years later. It is too much to imply that the play constitutes a prediction, but that aspect of it remains eerily prescient.

Cover of the programme for the Abbey Theatre. (*Courtesy of the Abbey Theatre*)

03

Seán MacDiarmada's Hurley
From GAA to IRB

Hurling is a game of great antiquity, but its status had declined in the decades after the catastrophic famine of the 1840s, as it was confined to pockets in Galway, Cork and Wexford. On the other hand, by the 1880s games such as soccer, rugby, cricket and golf were becoming increasingly popular and better organised across a wide social spectrum. In 1884 the Gaelic Athletic Association (GAA) was founded to provide a distinctively Irish alternative to these British imports. The key figure in its creation was Clare civil servant Michael Cusack, an athlete in his youth and an aficionado of cricket and rugby, who was nonetheless alarmed by the decline of 'native' games and the increasingly rapid spread of their British counterparts. The impetus for founding the GAA was, however, as much practical as ideological. Cusack and his close associate Maurice Davin worked off the assumption that the British rules which were increasingly used in Ireland for athletic competitions were just not suitable for Irish conditions. The British tradition of holding meetings on a Saturday, for instance, clashed with the more traditional Irish emphasis on sporting contests taking place on a Sunday.

The GAA was conceived of as a broad church and codified rules for the games under its aegis – initially hurling and athletics – had been developed by 1885. It grew rapidly, using parishes and counties as organisational units from an early stage. Eighty-four clubs were represented at the 1886 AGM that officially established the county boards and All-Ireland

championships, which first took place in 1887. Hurling and Gaelic football soon eclipsed athletics within the association.

The GAA had a broadly nationalist inflection from the outset, which ensured that the IRB had a presence in the organisation from an early stage. Consequently the authorities infiltrated it in turn, and although members of the armed forces were initially permitted to join, members of the Royal Irish Constabulary (RIC) were banned in 1887. By the end of the 1880s the GAA was effectively controlled by the IRB, a move which backfired disastrously when it became the only major national organisation to back the Home Rule leader Charles Stewart Parnell after his Irish Parliamentary Party split. This split was a result of the notorious O'Shea divorce case, in which Parnell had been named. The GAA then incurred the wrath of the Catholic Church, and was forced into a disastrous retreat in the 1890s. It recovered in the first decade of the twentieth century and naturally attracted the emerging generation of younger nationalists, such as Seán MacDiarmada, who apparently made the hurley pictured here.

MacDiarmada was born near Kiltyclogher in Co. Leitrim in 1883. His initial hopes to train as a teacher were scuppered due to his poor exam results in mathematics, but while working in Belfast he joined the IRB in 1906. He was appointed to a full-time position as an organiser, and after 1908 became the national organiser. He traversed the country discreetly seeking recruits for the brotherhood, with a particular emphasis on placing members in key positions within other nationalist organisations. Cultural nationalism, as manifested in numerous organisations, enjoyed broad support amongst many nationalists. It was argued by some more radical nationalists that if such groups were asserting that Ireland was culturally distinct from Britain, then surely it was only a short step towards asserting that Ireland should be politically separate. Not everyone took this position, but figures like Tom Clarke and MacDiarmada certainly espoused the view that organisations such as the GAA and others could be vehicles for the ambitions of the IRB. This is not to say that playing Gaelic games was just a cover for political activities, far from it, but the IRB sought to infiltrate the GAA and other cultural organisations with the intention of discreetly fostering support for separatism within their ranks. Given the nationalistic ethos of groups like the GAA, it was understandable that the IRB would view them as fertile ground for the reception of their ideals.

MacDiarmada was an active member of the GAA, but he contracted polio in 1911 and thereafter walked with a limp and required a walking stick. Presumably his active participation on the field ended after his illness, but along with Clarke, with whom he was closely associated, MacDiarmada drove forward the plan for another republican rebellion. '[A]s Clarke was the mastermind behind the Easter Rising, MacDiarmada was the master machinist, the man who more than any other assembled and manipulated the various cogs of organisation.'[1] MacDiarmada was a natural conspirator, articulate and charming, with little time for other ideologies that might distract from the central republican goal. In that sense he was akin to Clarke, but they also shared an obsession with secrecy that backfired disastrously in April 1916.

Seán MacDiarmada
(*Courtesy of Mercier Archive*)

---

1 Laurence White, 'Seán MacDiarmada', in *Dictionary of Irish Biography* (9 vols, Cambridge, 2009).

04

An Scoláire: St Enda's Student Magazine

A School for Revolution

An Scoláire was the student magazine of St Enda's College – Scoil Éanna – which opened in Dublin in September 1908 as an alternative to the state educational system that Patrick Pearse, its headmaster, famously castigated. Pearse became one of the public faces of the Easter Rising, but had this not happened, he would probably be remembered instead for his activism in the service of the Irish language and his pioneering educational experiment. The school received enthusiastic support from parents active in cultural nationalist circles, and even garnered the unlikely admiration of figures such as Robert Baden-Powell, who in 1909 tried to persuade Pearse to establish a branch of his Boy Scouts in Ireland. Yet as an avowed British imperialist, Baden-Powell was unlikely to have approved of the ethos of Pearse's school – it had been established in opposition to the influence of British imperial culture in Ireland (though Pearse was also critical of the teaching methods of the explicitly nationalistic Christian Brothers). At the same time, Pearse adapted elements of that same imperial culture, but gave them a distinctively Irish inflection, most notably in terms of idealising concepts of manliness and manhood, which was reflected in the school's emphasis on physical activity. Many of the extracurricular activities in the school placed a great emphasis on the mythological warriors of ancient Ireland, such as Cú Chulainn, and reflected a broader admiration for what was perceived to be the culture of Christian, pre-conquest Ireland.

"OUR-SUNDAY-VISITORS"

"Has "An Scoláire" come to stay?" Such is question of the hour. Some cranky critics answer "NO!"; some natures, optimistic, "Yes". However, that does not matter. Our first number was a success, even though it was issued on the fatal thirteenth. May this, the second, have the fate of the first. The Students were asked to contribute and support. They have acquitted themselves of the task in a manner honourable to their talents

The Irish language was a crucial part of the St Enda's curriculum, and Pearse was heavily influenced by continental models of bilingual teaching, as well as similar forms of cultural activism in Scotland and Wales. St Enda's was a boarding school, which adopted a child-centred model with a great emphasis on cultural, physical and artistic activities beyond the classroom, such as plays and pageantry. There was also an emphasis on practical activity: *An Scoláire* was handwritten by the students and mechanically reproduced in editions of fifty. The magazine contained a wide range of articles and verse in English, Irish and sometimes even French.

As time went by a more militant inflection crept into the curriculum of St Enda's. There was a natural crossover, for example, between Pearse's vision and Na Fianna Éireann, the republican scout group founded by Bulmer Hobson and Constance Markievicz in 1909. Indeed, Con Colbert of the Fianna (who was executed after the Easter Rising) was at one stage employed at St Enda's as a physical education instructor and surreptitiously recruited some of the students into the IRB. The issue of *An Scoláire* pictured here depicts the Fianna – described as 'our Sunday visitors' – on its front cover.

St Enda's was originally based at Cullenswood House in Ranelagh, before Pearse moved the school to the Hermitage in 1910–11. This was a larger premises in Rathfarnham, originally built in the eighteenth century as a house set in parkland (it now contains the Pearse Museum). After the move Cullenswood House became St Ita's, established by Pearse as a short-lived girls' school with a similar ethos to St Enda's. Although the move might imply that the school was a resounding success, Pearse was plagued by financial problems as he sought to keep his show on the road. The peak of St Enda's success was, in fact, in 1909–10 when 130 boys were enrolled; this dropped to seventy the following year.

From 1912 Pearse was beginning to turn his attention to more political matters. The activities of the school were overtaken by events, but a substantial number of its alumni were active in both the Easter Rising and the subsequent independence movement. St Enda's survived until 1935, but its heyday was long past by then.

The Hermitage: St Enda's College.
(*Courtesy of the Pearse Museum*)

05

A Bill from St Enda's to Éamonn Ceannt

Reviving a Language

Éamonn Ceannt was born Edward Kent in Glenamaddy, Co. Galway, in 1881, the son of a constable in the RIC. He grew up in Louth and Dublin, attending, like many others involved in the Rising, the Christian Brothers' O'Connell School on Richmond Street, in Dublin's north inner-city. After he graduated, he worked as a clerk for Dublin Corporation, and was one of the numerous young nationalists energised by the 1898 centenary of the United Irishmen's rebellion. He began to learn Irish (his father was a native speaker and helped him) and joined the Gaelic League. By 1909 Ceannt was on its governing body. Having adopted the Irish version of his own name, Ceannt fought a three-year campaign, after the birth of his only son, Ronan, in 1906, to permit his name to be registered in Irish. It is therefore not a surprise that Ceannt made a point of sending Ronan to St Enda's College.

The British authorities in Ireland never officially used the Irish language. Statistics for language proficiency were first incorporated into the 1851 census, and these revealed that Ireland in the immediate aftermath of the 1840s famine was a predominantly English-speaking country. The creation of the National School system in the 1830s had been followed by an observable increase in literacy levels in English in the second half of the nineteenth century (Irish was not officially part of the curriculum until 1878). However, this increasing proficiency in English was taking root at the same time as the usage of Irish was declining. By 1851 (according to

CULLENSWOOD HOUSE
(Oakley Road),
RATHMINES, Ráṫ Ṡeaṗnáin
DUBLIN.
Telephone 164 Rathmines.

Teaċ Ḟeaḋa Ċuilinn,
Ráṫ Ó Máine,
Baile Áṫa Cliaṫ,

II Meiṫeaṁ 1914

Éamonn Ceannt,

Bláṫ-Ġort, Carn na gCloċ.

I bḞiaċaiḃ le **Sġoil Éanna.**

To ST. ENDA'S SCHOOL, Dr.

1914		£ s d
Feaḃ. 1	Sgolaireaċt Rónáin go 19/6/14	2 10 0
	Lón gaċ lá	18 9
	Leaḃra ⁊c.:	
	Leaḃra Gaeḋilge	2
	" Béarla	2
	" Cleaċtaí	2
	" Nótaí	2
	" Sgríḃneoireaċta	2
	Teagasg Críostaiḋe	½
	Mion-ṗuisaí eile	1½
		1 0
		£3 9 9
M.fíġ. 8	Fríoṫ airgeas	£3 9 9

Maille le níoṗ-insar.

Éamonn Ceannt
(*private collection*)

the census of that year) less than 25 per cent of the population spoke Irish: 319,602 (4.88 per cent) were monoglot speakers, and 1,204,683 (18.38 per cent) were bilingual. The majority of Irish speakers were concentrated in the poor rural west, with pockets elsewhere. Clearly Irish was in decline, and this decline accelerated in the second half of the nineteenth century at an alarming rate. By 1891 approximately 15 per cent of the population spoke Irish and it was slowly but surely retreating westwards, where it remained a vernacular in substantial regions of the impoverished western seaboard.

The decline of the Irish language, and the loss of the vernacular culture that was expressed through Irish, came to be seen as a loss that was to be understood in qualitative rather than quantitative ways, and calls for a remedy became increasingly frequent. Attempts to revive Irish as a vernacular did not constitute a single coherent movement. The revival of Irish, alongside the increasing popularity of the GAA, became one of the most obvious markers of the late-nineteenth-century cultural revival, and by the end of the century Irish had secured an official foothold within the educational system.

For men like Ceannt the language was a fundamental element of their identity and he sought to ensure that his own son would know it; hence the choice of St Enda's. While being teetotal and a devout Catholic, Ceannt was also quite cosmopolitan, an accomplished piper and had an interest in foreign languages. His political beliefs were sufficiently militant to bring him to the attention of Seán MacDiarmada, who ushered him into the inner circle of the IRB which planned the Rising.

Ceannt was executed for his part in the Rising that broke out on 24 April 1916. On 24 April 1917 his brother William, a sergeant-major in the Royal Dublin Fusiliers, was killed on the Western Front; two brothers who died fighting very different wars.

06

The Ulster Covenant, 1912

ULSTER UNIONISM AND RESISTANCE TO HOME RULE

While the Easter Rising was carried out by separatist republicans, the vast majority of Irish people in 1916 were not republicans. The political cause that essentially had a monopoly on the hearts and minds of nationalist Ireland was that of Home Rule. This was the demand for limited Irish self-government within the United Kingdom that came to prominence from the late 1870s under the leadership of the Wicklow landlord Charles Stewart Parnell. However, for many in Britain, especially within the ranks of the Conservative Party, Irish Home Rule was a dangerous idea and one to be opposed, not least because it was seen as a potential danger to the Empire as a whole (even assuming that the Irish were capable of governing themselves; there was often a racist undertone to the debate). This opposition did not just come from Britain. The document pictured here – the Solemn League and Covenant of 1912 – is a small, yet visceral, reminder that a proportion of Ireland's population in the second decade of the twentieth century also held beliefs that were profoundly hostile to separatism in any form.

Home Rule Bills failed to pass through the Westminster parliament in 1886 and 1893. However, although Parnell had died in disgrace in 1891 after being named in the acrimonious O'Shea divorce case, the push for Home Rule did not die with him. By the second decade of the twentieth century Parnell's old party, the Irish Parliamentary Party, was being led by

Ulster's Solemn League and Covenant.

Being convinced in our consciences that Home Rule would be disastrous to the material well-being of Ulster as well as of the whole of Ireland, subversive of our civil and religious freedom, destructive of our citizenship and perilous to the unity of the Empire, we, whose names are underwritten, men of Ulster, loyal subjects of His Gracious Majesty King George V., humbly relying on the God whom our fathers in days of stress and trial confidently trusted, do hereby pledge ourselves in solemn Covenant throughout this our time of threatened calamity to stand by one another in defending for ourselves and our children our cherished position of equal citizenship in the United Kingdom and in using all means which may be found necessary to defeat the present conspiracy to set up a Home Rule Parliament in Ireland. ¶ And in the event of such a Parliament being forced upon us we further solemnly and mutually pledge ourselves to refuse to recognise its authority. ¶ In sure confidence that God will defend the right we hereto subscribe our names. ¶ And further, we individually declare that we have not already signed this Covenant.

The above was signed by me at _____
"Ulster Day," Saturday, 28th September, 1912.

God Save the King.

the Wexford MP John Redmond, a firm advocate of Ireland remaining within the British Empire, but with a government in Dublin. Redmond enjoyed virtually unchallenged support amongst Irish nationalists. He was also in a very strong position in Westminster, given that Herbert Asquith's government ruled with the support of eighty-four Irish nationalist MPs. It was inevitable that he would demand a third Home Rule Bill and so it proved. The third Home Rule Bill was passed by the House of Commons in 1912 amidst great jubilation in Ireland (though its implementation was delayed by the House of Lords for two years).

There was, however, one very significant catch. Most Irish nationalists may not have been republicans, but a quarter of the Irish population were not even nationalists. Irish unionism – the demand to maintain the union between Britain and Ireland as established in 1801 – had emerged during the 1880s in response to the increasing demands for Home Rule. While most Irish Catholics were nationalist in their politics, the majority of Irish Protestants were unionists who wanted to keep the link to Britain intact (though there were exceptions). On the eve of the First World War Protestants – mostly Anglicans and Presbyterians – made up approximately 26 per cent of the Irish population. They were overwhelmingly concentrated in the north-east of the country, but thinly dispersed throughout the rest of the island.

Protestants were hostile to the idea of Home Rule because, as a minority, they feared discrimination at the hands of a Dublin government dominated by the Catholic majority. As one of the most famous slogans of the era claimed, they believed Home Rule would also be Rome rule. In the north-east there were also fears that a Dublin-based government would endanger the industrial wealth of the region. After Asquith's government introduced the third Home Rule Bill in 1912, unionists in Ulster mobilised in spectacular style. In September 1912 over 237,000 unionist Ulstermen signed the Solemn League and Covenant that unequivocally stated their opposition to Home Rule in the strongest terms. Over 234,000 Protestant unionist women signed a declaration to the same effect. Unionism could be found all over Ireland, but it was obvious that Irish unionism was strongest in the Protestant heartlands of Ulster, and this was reflected once again by the creation, in early 1913, of the Ulster Volunteer Force (UVF).

The purpose of the UVF was to resist Home Rule, by force if need be. The threat of violence was implied in the stances taken by unionist leaders such as the Dublin lawyer Edward Carson and the Belfast business magnate James Craig. The UVF exploited various legal loopholes to permit the establishment of a private militia. Similar organisations sprang up in other parts of Ireland, but the UVF dwarfed any other such grouping. On the eve of the First World War it had perhaps as many as 90,000 members and had imported large quantities of weapons from Germany. It was also able to draw upon the experience of unionists who had served in the British Army and on the sympathy of many in British public life (up to and including the Conservative leader Andrew Bonar Law). If the impasse over Home Rule had created a political crisis in Ireland, then the creation of the UVF upped the ante significantly by rapidly militarising Irish politics, setting a precedent for others to follow.

07

Irish Citizen Army Flag

Class Conflict in the Irish Revolution

The Irish Citizen Army (ICA) was a trade union militia created during the 1913 Lockout – the popular name for the labour dispute orchestrated in Dublin by the union organiser James Larkin to resist attempts made by Dublin employers to bar members of his Irish Transport and General Workers' Union (ITGWU) from employment. The existence of the ICA is a reminder that the dominance of the 'national question' in Irish political life did not mean that other ideologies were absent from the Ireland of 1916. The iconic flag of the ICA featured the plough and the stars, later used as the title for Sean O'Casey's acerbic play featuring characters who are members of the ICA; the last acts of the play are set during the Rising.

In 1913 Dublin officially had a greater proportion of its population living in poverty than any other city in the United Kingdom – 87,000 out of a population of 304,000 – and urban poverty was exacerbated by relatively high levels of unskilled workers within the Dublin labour force. Larkin's attempts to organise the vast ranks of the unskilled labouring poor met with a ferocious response from Dublin's employers. After the transport magnate William Martin Murphy banned his employees from membership of the ITGWU in August 1913, Larkin called his union out on strike. Murphy galvanised other Dublin employers into a collective opposition to 'Larkinism', and the strike and Lockout snowballed into an industrial dispute that lasted until early 1914. It highlighted potent and enduring class tensions in Ireland that the focus on British rule often caused to be overlooked. By the end of September troops were being drafted in to protect property and guarantee supplies to government agencies, while shipments of food, organised by English unions, began to arrive in Dublin for the strikers and their families. Interestingly this British solidarity and aid was mistrusted by Seán MacDiarmada, but Patrick Pearse sympathised with Larkin's genuine demand for social and economic justice. By December the strikers had effectively been starved into submission, and the Lockout petered out in the early months of 1914. The employers insisted that those returning to work sign a pledge repudiating the ITGWU. However, the union survived.

So did the ICA, the foundation of which had been publicly proposed by James Connolly in November 1913 as a militia to protect strikers and union members from attacks by police and strike-breakers. Such attacks had accompanied the Lockout from its inception, most notoriously when Larkin addressed a crowd from the balcony of the Imperial Hotel on Sackville Street in August 1913. Connolly explicitly invoked the UVF as a precedent that Dublin workers might follow for their own protection. Other figures involved in the early incarnations of the ICA were the Home Ruler Jack White (who, having served in the British Army, put his own military experience at the disposal of the new organisation) and the future playwright Sean O'Casey.

James Connolly, who became the public face of the ICA in the years before 1916, was a committed socialist, who seems to have taken the view that a revolt against British rule could be the first blow in a war against capitalism. For Connolly, Irish independence would mark the beginning of a revolution rather than an end in itself (though it is debatable whether the rank and file of the ICA were doctrinaire socialists). The ICA was relatively small – it had only 334 members in early 1916 – and drew its strength from a poorer demographic than other paramilitary groups, such as the Irish Volunteers; the flag was, therefore, of more importance than a uniform that many of its members could not afford. It was first flown

over Liberty Hall in April 1914. The plough could be seen as a symbol of labour, with the constellation of Ursa Major representing aspiration, though Connolly himself apparently said that it represented an Ireland which would be free from the plough to the stars. The presence of a broken sword implies that the sword might yet be turned into a ploughshare. The design is sometimes credited to Belfast artist William Megahy.

The socialist beliefs of Connolly and his followers were not shared by the more conservative nationalists who were involved in the Rising, and class tensions made for uneasy bedfellows. When Mary MacSwiney in Cork heard rumours of the ICA's role in the outbreak of the Rising, she asked, 'was a fine body of men like the Irish Volunteers to be dragged at the tail of a rabble like the Citizen Army?'[1] Such tensions were a persistent theme throughout the revolutionary period, but there are undoubtedly links between 1913 and 1916. In the early phases of the Rising, ICA members killed two

Seán Connolly (no relation to James) of the ICA killed the man usually assumed to be the first victim of the Rising: DMP Constable James O'Brien, a native of Limerick who was shot dead at the gate to the Upper Castle Yard of Dublin Castle. Connolly himself was then fatally wounded by gunfire while on the roof of Dublin City Hall later that day. Had he not been involved in the Rising, Connolly was to have acted in a production of W. B. Yeats' play *Cathleen Ní Houlihan* at the Abbey Theatre on the evening of 24 April 1916.

(*private collection*)

---

1   Charles Townshend, *Easter 1916: the Irish Rebellion* (London, 2005), pp. 235–6.

members of the Dublin Metropolitan Police (DMP) and they may well have been settling scores left over from the earlier Lockout. There was a symbolic echo of 1913 as well: during the Rising Connolly instructed that the Citizen Army flag be flown over the Imperial Hotel on Sackville Street, presumably for the same reason that Larkin had spoken from its balcony in August 1913: the owner of the Imperial Hotel was none other than their great adversary William Martin Murphy. A cavalry officer, Lieutenant T. A. Williams, took the flag after the Rising; the National Museum obtained it from him in 1954.

Baton charge by the RIC on Sackville Street following Larkin's address in the Imperial Hotel. (*Courtesy of Mercier Archive*)

08

Diarmuid Lynch's Irish Volunteer Uniform

THE MILITARISATION OF IRISH NATIONALISM

On 1 November 1913 UCD historian Eoin MacNeill published an article entitled 'The North Began' in the Gaelic League newspaper *An Claidheamh Soluis*. This called on Irish nationalists to emulate the example of their unionist counterparts in the UVF, but to do so in order to defend Home Rule. The result was the foundation of the Irish Volunteers, who held their inaugural public meeting in Dublin's Rotunda Rink on 25 November 1913, attended by thousands. This new nationalist militia was larger than the UVF, perhaps numbering over 160,000 at its peak, though it was never as well equipped or well trained. However, some of its members, such as Diarmuid Lynch, were able to turn out in a proper Irish Volunteer uniform, and it is his uniform, pictured here, that is today preserved in the Cork Public Museum. Lynch was a Cork-born IRB member, who represented Munster on that organisation's supreme council, fought in the GPO during the Rising and later served as a Sinn Féin TD for Cork.

While the Irish Volunteers were founded in response to the UVF, their founding manifesto was at pains to point out that their real opponent was the Conservative Party ('one of the great English political parties') rather than the UVF. The Volunteers seemed wary of giving the impression that they were being set up to foment a sectarian war with the UVF; rather, their professed purpose was 'to secure and maintain the

Diarmuid Lynch
(*Courtesy of Mercier Archive*)

rights and liberties common to all the people of Ireland'.[1] Volunteer companies began to spring up across Ireland, often emerging from existing groups such as the Gaelic League, and often being drilled by nationalist ex-servicemen (one of the tools of the Volunteer's trade was the British Army's field manual). In political terms the Volunteers accommodated a wide range of beliefs, but the IRB was involved from the outset. The Belfast IRB leader Bulmer Hobson had been one of those to urge the foundation of the organisation and once that had happened it was discreetly infiltrated by the IRB, which sought to put its own members into positions of influence. As one IRB man, Gerald Byrne, later put it, 'this was a chance to do openly what we had previously to do in secret'.[2]

The Irish Volunteers had to have a credible public face, which meant trying to obtain weapons and uniforms; and the latter were easier to get than the former. The uniform was only agreed upon in August 1914 and was to be made of Irish cloth in Ireland (the first batch of uniforms was made in Dublin, with the cloth sourced in Cork). There was also a cap-badge designed by MacNeill, emblazoned with 'FF' (meaning Fianna Fáil, in a reference to the eponymous warriors of Irish mythology). Diarmuid Lynch could afford to

---

1 Townshend, *Easter 1916*, p. 41.
2 Fearghal McGarry, *Rebels: Voices from the Easter Rising* (London, 2011), p. 69.

purchase a uniform (though he was by no means a rich man), but many of the Volunteers could not; instead, Sam Browne belts with improvised and stylised buckles were worn over civilian clothing by many.

Regardless of how they were dressed, the Irish Volunteers were a seminal organisation in the Irish revolution: the north may well have begun, as MacNeill suggested, but it was the Volunteers who made the next move by militarising nationalist Ireland, and the organisation provided most of the foot soldiers for the Easter Rising. The existence of the Volunteers reflected the crisis over the question of Home Rule that had flared up after 1912. By the summer of 1914 it was obvious that the nationalist and unionist communities of Ireland had completely different visions of what Ireland's future should be, and before the outbreak of the First World War the prospect of civil war in Ireland was one of the dominant issues in the domestic politics of what was then the United Kingdom. The outbreak of a much larger conflict across the European continent in 1914 prevented this happening.

A group of Irish Volunteers on parade.
(*Courtesy of Kilmainham Gaol Museum, 16PC-1A43-07*)

09

Cumann na mBan Brooch
Irish Women and Irish Revolution

As an item of jewellery this brooch could be deemed to be purely decorative, but the fact that its design incorporates a rifle indicates that there is more to it than that.

The foundation of the Irish Volunteers inadvertently posed the question of how Irish women could be accommodated within the new militarism. From the 1870s onwards the question of conceding greater economic, educational and political rights to women had become more evident in Ireland (as in Britain). Progress was being made slowly on some of these fronts; women got the vote in local elections in 1898 and by 1911 could sit on county councils. However, women were still not permitted to vote in parliamentary elections (which prompted the foundation of the Irish Women's Franchise League in 1908) and mainstream Irish nationalists in the Home Rule party tended to be quite hostile to the idea of giving women the vote. It is hardly surprising then that, over time, some Irish women began to feel as if their own liberation as women was intertwined with the broader struggle for cultural and political independence.

Cumann na mBan (Irish Women's Council) was founded in Dublin in April 1914, at a meeting chaired by the UCD Irish lecturer Agnes O'Farrelly. There were debates over whether or not it was simply to act as a women's auxiliary to the Volunteers, but O'Farrelly argued persuasively that the new group should not be affiliated to any one party and Cumann na mBan came into existence as an organisation in its own right. It was

not the first organisation of its kind: Inghinidhe na hÉireann (Daughters of Ireland) was founded at the turn of the century as a cultural nationalist organisation for Irish women. One of its more famous activities was the organising of a 'Patriotic Children's Treat' – a picnic for children – in protest at the visit to Ireland of Queen Victoria in 1900, during the Second Boer War. The organisation was also involved in anti-recruiting activities. It had a very distinctive identity and sense of purpose, and aimed to both reflect the needs of Irishwomen and permit them to participate in cultural and political life. Helena Molony later described Inghinidhe na hÉireann's newspaper as 'a funny hotch-potch of blood and thunder, high thinking, and home-made bread'.[1]

Cumann na mBan was, in many ways, similar to Inghinidhe na hÉireann (which it replaced), but, in keeping with the era in which it was founded, it was more militant in both its outlook and rhetoric (as the brooch might suggest). Only a few months old when the First World War broke out, it aligned itself with those Volunteers who opposed John Redmond's call to support the war effort, and suffered near-fatal damage by losing many members in the process. However, the fledgling organisation survived and was reorganised, and before 1916, under the leadership of women such as Jennie Wyse-Power and Nancy O'Rahilly, it became more militant in both theory and practice.

Cumann na mBan was kept in the dark about the plans for the Rising, but members of the organisation were present in virtually all of the Dublin garrisons during the Rising, though not necessarily as active combatants. Many male republican activists, including Éamon de Valera, seem to have disapproved of the idea of Irish women fighting, so many ended up preparing food and supplies and tending to the wounded. Others acted as messengers and travelled between the various insurgent garrisons, displaying considerable courage as they did so.

---

1   McGarry, *Rebels*, p. 40.

In the aftermath of the Rising Cumann na mBan became prominent in propaganda and fund-raising activities for republican prisoners. The existence of Cumann na mBan gave Irish women a presence, and some degree of representation, within the independence movement that emerged after 1916.

Marcella Cosgrave, who was based in Jameson's Distillery on Marrowbone Lane during the Rising, in her Cumann na mBan uniform.
(*Courtesy of Kilmainham Gaol Museum, KMGLM 2012.0131*)

10

A Baton used in the Howth Gun-running

Raising the Stakes

Private militias such as the Irish Volunteers and the UVF counted for little without weapons. From December 1913 the importation of weapons into the UK had been made illegal, but in April 1914 the UVF successfully landed 25,000 rifles and a substantial quantity of ammunition (purchased in Germany) at the northern port of Larne. The Irish Volunteers soon followed suit, albeit on a much smaller scale. The former British consular official and Irish nationalist Sir Roger Casement contacted sympathetic figures based in London, such as the Anglo-Irish Mary Spring Rice, and this circle was then widened to include Eoin MacNeill, Bulmer Hobson and former British naval officer Erskine Childers. They raised the requisite sum of money to purchase a consignment of rifles and ammunition in Hamburg, and in July 1914 these weapons were smuggled into Ireland in two shipments.

The first, larger and most public shipment of 900 rifles was brought to the fishing village of Howth, north of Dublin, on Childers' yacht, *Asgard*. The weapons were single-shot Mauser rifles dating from the 1870s: old and loud, but accurate and perfectly serviceable. However, the weapons could not simply be dumped on the pier at Howth; they would have to be collected, and so members of the Irish Volunteers and the Fianna travelled out to Howth to meet the *Asgard*. Amongst them was the railway clerk and Fianna leader Seán Heuston, whose inner-city detachment of Fianna possessed a simple, two-wheeled collapsible cart that could be used to

Gordon Shepard and Erskine Childers on board the *Asgard*. Note the crate of ammunition on the left.
(*Courtesy of Mercier Archive*)

transport their equipment. They assembled on the morning of 26 July; Heuston told the members of his detachment (or sluagh) that their heavily laden cart contained refreshments (he didn't go into specifics) before they started on their march to Howth.

When they arrived, the *Asgard* was berthed beside the lighthouse at the east pier of Howth Harbour. The Fianna were given the job of unloading its cargo and formed a human chain on the quayside. Heuston and a number of others jumped aboard the yacht and, as one of those present put it, 'almost at once, long rifles with gleaming barrels began to appear from the hold and were passed from hand to hand to the waiting men on the pier'.[1] Heuston instructed another group to load the hand cart with ammunition boxes that were being taken from the *Asgard*. By now the cart had been emptied of its original contents, which were not 'minerals' of any sort: it had been used to transport batons, such as the one pictured here, which were now in the hands of the Volunteers lining the approach to the east pier. These batons were to be used to protect them from any policemen who might interfere

---

1   John Gibney, *16 Lives: Seán Heuston* (Dublin, 2013), p. 67.

with the weapons being landed or confront them on their way back to the city.

The Volunteers and Fianna were not confronted by the authorities until they reached Fairview (12 km from Howth). There, they encountered the DMP (some members of which were apparently sympathetic to the gun-running) and soldiers (members of the King's Own Scottish Borderers) from the Royal Barracks, who demanded that they surrender the guns that had just been landed. This contrasted with the treatment of the UVF, who suffered no sanctions, despite importing a much larger shipment of weapons. In the resulting affray, two soldiers were injured and nineteen rifles were confiscated. Some members of the Fianna and Volunteers managed to flee the scene and hide the weapons. Heuston hid the hand cart in nearby Donnycarney. As they marched back to the Royal Barracks, the King's Own Scottish Borderers shot dead three people when they opened fire on a hostile crowd on Bachelor's Walk.

A second, smaller shipment of 600 rifles was landed at Kilcoole in Co. Wicklow a week later under cover of darkness. The arrival of these rifles suggested that the Irish Volunteers were becoming a force to take seriously; the batons had a short career as a stop gap.

Teresa Reddin of Cumann na mBan leads the funeral procession for the victims of the Bachelor's Walk shootings. (*Courtesy of Kilmainham Gaol Museum, 16PO-1A-09*)

11

Irish National Volunteers Uniform

THE GREAT WAR AND THE VOLUNTEER SPLIT

The name of the Irish Volunteers is quite well known; that of the Irish National Volunteers, less so. Yet at one time the former vastly outnumbered the latter. The distinction arose from the split that took place in the Volunteers after the outbreak of the First World War in August 1914, which also defused the Home Rule crisis in Ireland. Home Rule became law on 18 September 1914, but with the caveat that it was to be postponed for a year (or until the war was over), and that some provision for Protestant Ulster would be made (the partition of Ireland in 1920 was the eventual outcome). Once the long-standing demand for devolution was officially on the statute book, John Redmond, in a famous speech in Woodenbridge, Co. Wicklow, exhorted nationalists to enlist in the British Army and to serve 'as far as the firing line extended', as the war was being 'undertaken in defence of the highest principles of religion and morality and right'. Given that Germany had invaded (Catholic) Belgium, should Irishmen not fight, argued Redmond, it would be 'a disgrace forever to our country' and 'a denial of the lessons of her history'.[1]

Redmond's support for the war effort prompted a catastrophic split in the Irish Volunteers, as it brought to a head tensions that had been simmering ever since he had sought to exert control over the organisation earlier in the summer. People like Eoin MacNeill essentially repudiated

---

1 *The Freeman's Journal*, 21 September 1914.

Redmond's claim to authority over the Volunteers, but this proved to be a miscalculation, as the vast majority of the original organisation chose to follow Redmond and adopted the name Irish National Volunteers. A smaller faction who opposed the war effort retained the original name (perhaps only 9,700 out of 156,000 remained within the Irish Volunteers), and provided most of the manpower for the rebellion that broke out in April 1916.

The outbreak of the Great War also provided the pretext for the Easter Rising. When Gearóid O'Sullivan told Seán MacDiarmada of the assassination of Archduke Franz Ferdinand, after hearing of it from a newsboy on a Dublin street, MacDiarmada immediately exclaimed, 'Look it Gearóid, this is no joke for us. We're in for it now. Austria will move against these fellows ... Russia will back these fellows up, Germany and Italy will back Austria, France will take on Germany. You'll have a European war; England will join – and that will be our time to strike.'[2]

MacDiarmada was right. In September 1914, within weeks of the outbreak of the war, a diverse assembly of militant nationalists met in Dublin and key figures amongst them, including Tom Clarke and MacDiarmada, resolved that they would exploit the opportunity presented by the war: England's difficulty was to be used as Ireland's opportunity. And so, in September 1914, Clarke and his fellow conspirators committed themselves to an uprising before the war ended.

On 17 April 1916 the British authorities estimated that the membership of the Irish Volunteers stood at 8,381; that of the Redmondite National Volunteers was estimated at 104,084. The difference in the size of the organisations is misleading, however, as the National Volunteers had lost their momentum and became increasingly inactive as the war progressed. The British, on the other hand, viewed the smaller Irish Vol-

---

2   R. F. Foster, *Vivid Faces: the Revolutionary Generation in Ireland, 1891–1923* (London, 2014), p. 177.

unteers as the most active, if poorly armed, paramilitary organisation on the island of Ireland before the Rising. They were right on both counts.

John Redmond overseeing the blessing of 'Drums and Colours' at an Irish National Volunteer Parade, *c.* 1914.
(*Courtesy of Mercier Archive*)

12

Manuscript of Patrick Pearse's Oration at the Funeral of Jeremiah O'Donovan Rossa, 1915

A Statement of Intent

One of the most telling events in the run-up to the Easter Rising was Patrick Pearse's famous (or infamous) oration at the grave of the veteran Fenian Jeremiah O'Donovan Rossa in Dublin's Glasnevin Cemetery on 1 August 1915. Jeremiah O'Donovan (he adopted 'Rossa' in later life) was born in Rosscarbery in Co. Cork in 1831. Deeply affected by the human horrors of the Great Famine in that region, he later worked in Skibbereen as a merchant and publican, and was active in the IRB from an early stage. O'Donovan Rossa was imprisoned in 1858 for Fenian activities, and his businesses fell foul of the Roman Catholic Church and local landlords, both of whom were hostile to the IRB for different reasons. Eventually moving to Dublin, he managed the Fenian newspaper *The Irish People*, before being arrested and sentenced to life imprisonment in 1865. He proved to be a difficult inmate and was treated harshly in the early years of his sentence. Released in 1871 on condition that he leave the UK, O'Donovan Rossa went to America and established his own newspaper, *United Irishman*. He advocated and orchestrated bombing campaigns in Britain in the 1880s. In the 1890s he visited Britain and returned to live in Ireland, before finally settling in New York in 1906, where he died in June 1915.

O'Donovan Rosa.
Funeral
~~Address~~ at Graveside.
P. H. Pearse.

It has been thought right, before we turn away from this place in which we have laid the mortal remains of O'Donovan Rossa, that one among us should, in the name of all, speak the praise of that valiant man, and endeavour to formulate the thought and the hope that are in us as we stand around his grave. And if there is anything that makes it fitting that I rather than another, & rather ~~~~ than one of the greyhaired men who were young with him and ~~~~ shared in his labour and in his suffering, should speak here, it is perhaps that I may be taken as speaking on behalf of a new generation that has been re-baptised in the Fenian faith and that has accepted the responsibility of carrying out the Fenian programme. I propose to you then that, here by the grave of this unrepentant Fenian, we renew our baptismal vows; that, here by the grave of this unconquered and unconquerable man, we ask of God, each one for himself, such unshakable purpose, such high and gallant courage, ~~~~ such unbreakable strength of soul as belonged to O'Donovan Rossa.

Deliberately ~~~~ here, we avow ourselves, as he avowed himself in the dock, Irishmen of one allegiance only. We of the Irish Volunteers and you others who are associ-

Jeremiah O'Donovan Rossa
(*Courtesy of Mercier Archive*)

O'Donovan Rossa had apparently expressed a wish to be buried in Ireland and the veteran Clan na Gael leader John Devoy decided to facilitate this. Tom Clarke also spotted an opportunity and a committee was convened to arrange what became a large and elaborate Fenian funeral. While he had come to be seen in some quarters as a vaguely pathetic figure in later life, O'Donovan Rossa's trenchant views, hostility to British authority in captivity and remarkable knack for invective and publicity ensured that he, and what he symbolised, was bound to attract attention. His body lay in state in Dublin City Hall before an enormous cortège, marshalled by the Irish Volunteers, made its way to Glasnevin Cemetery. After the funeral mass, a single speaker gave an oration: Patrick Pearse, in his Volunteer uniform, sprung a surprise on his listeners.

The speech, with its famous refrain 'the fools, the fools, the fools', was a very deliberate statement on behalf of the military council of the IRB, who were, at this time, planning what became the Easter Rising. While the preparations for the Rising were conducted in secret, Pearse's speech sought to bring the IRB out of the shadows via a very public assertion that in the Ireland of 1915 there were those who, as he put it, had 'been re-baptised in the Fenian faith'. It deliberately linked militant nationalism, in the form of the Irish Volunteers, with the older republican tradition exemplified by the IRB. The symbolic meaning was undeniable: one generation was receiving the baton of republican separatism from another, and the speech was deliberately conceived to fulfil this role. It is the most famous of Pearse's public pronouncements in the prelude to the Rising and is perhaps the most famous speech of that era. Pearse was unsure how far he should go, but on consulting Clarke about the tone he ought to strive for, he was encouraged not to hold back and to make the speech as 'hot as hell'.¹

The original text, pictured here, was drafted in Pearse's cottage in Rosmuc in the Connemara Gaeltacht. While Pearse's prose can often seem clunky and hyperbolic on the page, he had an undoubted gift for oratory and rhetoric. His tendency towards the bombastic – occasionally interspersed with some indefensible comments – makes him a natural figure to criticise. His firebreathing speeches are often assumed to have inspired many to get involved in paramilitarism of various kinds. Yet if making speeches that encouraged young men to fight for a cause is a criteria for criticism, it should be noted that Pearse's contemporaries Edward Carson and John Redmond – both of whom would have been listened to by a much larger audience than Pearse – were quite capable of making speeches that explicitly encouraged young Irish men of differing creeds and classes to enlist in the British Army. It was common for violence to be glorified in a world that was at war.

O'Donovan Rossa's funeral committee.
(*Courtesy of the National Library of Ireland*)

---

1 James Quinn, 'Thomas Clarke', in *Dictionary of Irish Biography*.

13

Uniform for Roger Casement's 'Irish Brigade'

Gallant Allies in Europe

The outbreak of war in 1914 had (as Seán MacDiarmada dramatically realised) offered the prospect of a marriage of convenience between the IRB and Germany. To that end, contact was made with the German authorities through John Devoy in New York and, in late 1914, Roger Casement travelled to Germany to secure their assistance. Casement had an internationally renowned (if contentious) career due to his investigations into the brutal treatment of indigenous populations in the Belgian Congo and in the Amazon basin by commercial rubber interests. He subsequently resigned from the British consular service and, returning to Ireland, became involved in the embryonic Irish Volunteers, before helping to organise the Howth gun-running of 1914.

Casement had become a critic of Britain's imperial ambitions, especially in relation to Germany. He anticipated that the Germans might aid the Irish cause in a number of ways by offering material assistance for a rebellion in Ireland, and also by permitting Casement to recruit an 'Irish Brigade' from amongst Irish soldiers in German captivity, who might be inclined to join such a rebellion. The object here is the uniform that they would have worn; a modified German army uniform, complete with Irish symbols, including harps and shamrocks.

Casement's plan quickly ran into difficulties. While there were large numbers of Irish prisoners in German custody, they were scattered across a

number of locations. Even aside from the logistics of trying to visit them to make his case, how was Casement to identify who might be inclined to join such a unit? Many, if not most, of these prisoners were nationalists, but that did not automatically guarantee that they would fight in a uniform supplied by Germany, even on purely pragmatic grounds. Casement's attempt to recruit his Irish Brigade was a miserable failure; few recruits came forward and, indeed, Casement was met with open hostility from Irish prisoners on at least one occasion. He recruited only fifty-five men and by April 1915 admitted to his German contacts that his proposal for an Irish Brigade was, in practical terms, a failure. This seems to have discredited him in German eyes. Equally, figures like Devoy, who remained a crucial conduit between Ireland and Germany, did not fully trust Casement's judgement and so he was left in the dark concerning the planning for the Rising that was underway.

Members of the Irish Brigade recruited from amongst Irish prisoners of war in German captivity by Roger Casement. Only a handful of recruits came forward. *Left to right*: David Golden, Michael Keogh, — O'Mahoney, Daniel Bailey, — Zerhussen (interpreter), — Kavanagh, — O'Callaghan, Timothy Quinlisk. (*Courtesy of Mercier Archive*)

Biscuit tin and biscuits from the *Aud*.
(*Courtesy of Cork Public Museum*)

The *Aud*. Originally a cargo ship called the *Castro*, it had been seized by the German authorities earlier in the war and was renamed the *Libau*. For the purposes of running guns to Ireland before Easter 1916, it was renamed the *Aud*, in order to disguise it as a neutral Norwegian vessel. (*Courtesy of Mercier Archive*)

have been readily available in Ireland; had the Volunteers actually received them, how long could they have lasted before they ran out of ammunition?

Having travelled a circuitous route through the North Sea, the *Aud* reached the Irish coast, but could not communicate with the Irish Volunteers who were meant to rendezvous with it. The mobilisation and movement of Volunteers in Cork, Kerry and Limerick at Easter 1916 was, as far as many of those involved were concerned, geared towards receiving the weapons rather than carrying out an immediate insurrection. The idea was that if the weapons were landed in north Kerry, the Volunteers could (and would) take control of Tralee and Listowel. A train would then be commandeered to travel up the west coast, distributing the weapons in Limerick, Clare and east Galway. However, the inability to communicate with the ship, which lacked a radio, combined with uncertainty as to when it was actually going to arrive, guaranteed that the weapons were never landed.

On 22 April 1916 the *Aud* was intercepted by the Royal Navy and scuttled by its crew near Queenstown (Cobh). The failure of the gun-running crippled even the limited prospect of a substantial rebellion taking place; without weapons what could any prospective insurgents do? The Volunteers' chief of staff, Eoin MacNeill, had been made aware of the IRB's plans for the Rising only in the days before its outbreak (he opposed the idea of Irish Volunteers fighting unless in very limited and exceptional circumstances), and the news that this attempt to import weapons had failed led him to conclude that the rebellion was doomed to failure. It also caused the British authorities to realise that the fringe nationalist organisations they had been prepared to tolerate would finally have to be dealt with.

The fact that this rifle never fired a shot in Ireland not only scuppered one possible version of the Easter Rising – it indirectly defined the nature and extent of the Rising that began on 24 April 1916.

The car that drove off Ballykissane Pier in Co. Kerry on 21 April 1916. It was carrying four members of the Irish Volunteers who were planning on making contact with the *Aud*; three of the four men were drowned. (*Courtesy of Mercier Archive*)

15

Teacups used by the Pearse Brothers
Calm before the Storm

These teacups and saucers were apparently used by Patrick and Willie Pearse at the last family meal they had at St Enda's before going out to take part in the Easter Rising. They can be seen as quintessentially middle class, which is perhaps an appropriate description for the Pearse family as a whole. Patrick, born in 1879, was the eldest of the two boys born to James and Margaret Pearse. Their father was a stonemason and sculptor, originally from London, who ran a successful business in Dublin. Patrick attended UCD and was an enthusiast for the Irish language from an early age. He trained to be a barrister, but had no taste for the profession and instead ended up working for the Gaelic League, editing (and writing a great deal of) its newspaper, *An Claidheamh Soluis*.

Patrick Pearse is, for many people, the public face of the Easter Rising, and he left behind a litany of often extreme rhetoric, publicly expressed with unwavering certainty. His indefensible statement that 'the old heart of the earth needed to be warmed with the red wine of the battlefields', made in December 1915, was hardly likely to endear him or his cause to those who had been maimed or bereaved by the First World War. Yet such utterances can obscure the fact that in many ways Pearse was a progressive and pragmatic intellectual; the foundation of St Enda's being the most obvious example of this. While he publicly eulogised a mythical version of the Gaelic past, he did so largely for polemical purposes; privately Pearse felt that any revival of Irish would have to be as a modern language,

appropriate to the twentieth century in which he and his generation lived. He was no insular bigot; he was both humane and cosmopolitan. The practical application of his bilingual education philosophy, as practised in St Enda's, was modelled on the Belgian school system, and he eschewed corporal punishment for the students.

In political terms, Pearse had supported Home Rule as late as 1912, but became disillusioned and radicalised in subsequent years. He remained interested in Home Rule even after he joined the IRB in December 1913, but his public writings also reveal a commitment to separatism, though he seemed flexible as to how such separation might be achieved. Pearse's knack for rhetorical flourishes brought him to the attention of Tom Clarke, who gladly let him become the public face of republican militancy during the First World War. Pearse rapidly rose through the ranks of the Irish Volunteers, becoming their director of military organisation in December 1914. Having made a rapid transition from cultural and educational activism to militant separatism, he became central to the planning of the Easter Rising.

It is sometimes suggested, based on a reading of Pearse's speeches and poems in which he glorified self-sacrifice, that the Easter Rising can be seen as some kind of sacrificial gesture, where Ireland would be resurrected at Easter just like Jesus Christ. This obscures the fact that Pearse and his co-conspirators had devised elaborate plans for their rebellion; martyrdom need not require such planning. Some contemporaries felt that Pearse and others were prepared to sacrifice themselves. Even if that is true, the impulse could surely co-exist with a desire to succeed, but by the time that Patrick Pearse finished his tea and put down his cup for the last time, he could have been under no illusion as to what was likely to happen to him if – when – the rebellion was defeated.

Patrick Pearse
(*private collection*)

Patrick usually overshadows his younger brother Willie. Born in 1881, Willie was a talented sculptor who trained in Dublin, London and Paris, and eventually took over their father's business. While the firm was still commissioned to produce pieces (such as the 'Mater Dolorosa' in St Andrew's church on Westland Row in Dublin, apparently a particular favourite of Willie's), it closed in 1910. Willie was active in the Gaelic League and taught at both St Enda's and St Ita's. He also joined the Irish Volunteers, but, while he fought in the Rising, he played no role in the planning. It is often assumed that his eventual execution was vindictive – that he was executed because of his surname. The reality was that Willie Pearse was the only one of the men executed in Dublin after the Rising to plead guilty to the charges laid before him. He was shot in Kilmainham Gaol on 4 May 1916, the day after Patrick was executed.

These teacups are a prosaic, and indeed humble, link to ordinary life before the upheaval of April 1916; for the remaining members of the Pearse family they were also a link to the two sons or brothers that they had lost. According to Margaret Pearse, their sister, the last conversation she ever had with her brothers came after they had tea, presumably from these cups, on the weekend before the Rising. W. B. Yeats' famous observation in his poem 'Easter 1916' that all was 'changed utterly' is correctly taken to be a commentary on Irish public affairs in the aftermath of the Rising. Yet it is also applicable in private terms to those families, such as the Pearses, who were irrevocably changed by the loss of those members killed during, and in this case because of, the Easter Rising.

Willie Pearse
(*Courtesy of Mercier Archive*)

16

Mobilisation Order for 'B' Company, 1st Battalion, Dublin Brigade, Irish Volunteers, 24 April 1916

THE RISING BEGINS

On Easter Monday 1916 this small slip of paper was issued to mobilise a member of B Company of the 1st Battalion of the Dublin Brigade of the Irish Volunteers, led by Edward Daly. It came a day late, as the architects of the Rising sought to salvage something from the wreckage of plans that had fallen apart spectacularly in the days before Easter 1916.

The Rising was originally meant to begin on Easter Sunday, when the Irish Volunteers were to assemble for regular weekend manoeuvres and would then be informed of the rebellion. Tom Clarke's obsession with secrecy meant that the rank and file were kept in the dark until the last minute, though many suspected that something was being planned (and accepted that the ultimate purpose of the Volunteers was 'a belt at the bloody British').[1] But the loss of the *Aud* convinced Eoin MacNeill, who had only been made aware of the plans on 20 April, that any rebellion was doomed to failure. He attempted to call it off by cancelling the Volunteer manoeuvres scheduled for Easter Sunday; the rank and file were none the wiser.

---

1   National Library of Ireland (NLI) MS 36,147: Patrick J. Stephenson, 'Heuston's Fort: the Mendicity Institute, Easter Week 1916' [1966].

IRISH VOLUNTEERS.
DUBLIN BRIGADE.

The......B......Coy., ...1st......

of......11-30...... m.

Point of Mobilisation......B......

Full Service Equipment to be
bottle, canteen.

Rations for............................

Cycle Scouts to be mounted, and
bring them.

Dated this......24......day of......

ANY MOBILISATION ORDER.

...Batt., will mobilise to-day at the hour

........*David Phelan*........

including overcoat, haversack, water-

to be carried.

men having cycles or motor cycles to

........*d Lieut*........

aptain or Officer Commanding.

........, 191...

Clarke, Patrick Pearse and the other leaders were now deprived not just of the weapons on the *Aud*, but also of the numbers they had hoped to mobilise. They also faced the prospect that the attempt to import weapons might trigger a British crackdown that would deprive them of even a limited opportunity for insurrection. And so the rebel leaders went ahead with their plan. It seems that the overwhelming sentiment amongst those who took part in the Rising was that it was better to act quickly rather than lose their opportunity – better to do something, no matter how foolhardy, than nothing.

Were the rebels intent on success, or simply upon martyrdom? The answer lies somewhere in between. The idea of becoming a martyr for Ireland and the idea of actually being involved in a successful rebellion were not mutually exclusive. Fearghal McGarry's characterisation of it as 'armed propaganda' is reasonable.[2] In the eyes of many of those who took part, the Rising was more of an effort to maintain the integrity of the marginalised separatist tradition than a foolhardy attempt to emulate Christ on the cross. The subsequent recasting of 1916 as a spiritual or metaphysical struggle, in which victory did not matter, was simply a handy way of getting around the awkward reality of military defeat. It also overlooks the preparations that went into the Rising.

Some of the testimonies collated after the event reveal the outline of two risings: one in Dublin, arguably for propaganda purposes, that went ahead; one in the provinces, that did not. Yet even if more men had turned up on Easter Monday, what weapons were they to use? The local Volunteers who seized Enniscorthy in Wexford, for example, were so desperate for weapons that they had manufactured pikes. Even if weapons from the *Aud* had been landed and distributed along the west coast in Cork, Kerry,

---

2 Fearghal McGarry, 'Easter Rising (Great Britain and Ireland)', in *International Encyclopedia of the First World War* (http://encyclopedia.1914-1918-online.net/article/easter_rising_great_britain_and_ireland).

Clare, Limerick and Galway, as was apparently meant to happen, members of the Volunteers in those counties seem to have been unclear as to what they were supposed to do when they received them. In Cork city, many of the Volunteers who assembled on Easter Sunday ultimately ended up going home. The mere existence of a plan does not mean that it was a plan that had been fully worked out; it does, however, cast doubt on the well-worn notion that the Rising was a form of self-sacrifice.

There were aspects of the Rising that made good sense and had obviously been well thought out. Volunteer units outside Dublin, for instance, were given specific instructions to cut rail links to hamper the movement of British forces to Dublin. Within the city, B Company of the 1st Battalion of the Dublin Volunteers – the recipients of mobilisation orders such as the one pictured here – were instructed to seize and, if possible, destroy the bridges over the Midlands Great Western Railway at the North Circular Road and Cabra. Had the line been blocked, it would have been an impediment to the arrival of reinforcements from British garrisons in the midlands and the west of Ireland. The loss of the bridges would also have hampered troops from Marlborough Barracks moving into the north inner-city. The theory, at least, was sound.

The Rising that broke out may not have been the Rising that was anticipated, but the defeat came down to one simple factor: the willingness of the British to use overwhelming force to defeat it. Even had there been a more substantial and sustained uprising around the country, the British simply would not – could not – have tolerated it in a time of war, and would almost certainly have crushed it accordingly. In that sense, the seven men who put their names to the Proclamation can have had few illusions about what their eventual fate would be.

17

A Poster for the Coliseum Theatre, 24 April 1916

A Day Like Any Other

Monday 24 April 1916 was a public holiday. For most Dubliners, and indeed most Irish people, it should have been no different from other public holidays. At least some of them were probably planning a trip to the Coliseum Theatre to see the acts listed on this poster.

The Coliseum was a variety theatre on Henry Street, very well appointed and with an unusually large stage. With a capacity of 3,000, it was a substantial addition to Dublin's theatres. It opened on Easter Monday 1915; an irony, in light of its eventual fate. The opening night went well, though the rendition of a recruiting song entitled 'Your Country Wants You' prompted one wag seated behind the theatre critic Joseph Holloway to quip that 'it does, and we intend to stop it'.[1] Discontent in the audience was magnified when the first bars of 'God Save the King' were played, and the anthem was discreetly abandoned for the second house at 9 p.m.

The Coliseum did not automatically cater for Irish performers: the emphasis was on touring companies, which was perhaps a consequence – and perhaps a necessity – arising from its size. The punters who were supposed to fill it on the evening of 24 April were presumably surprised by the occupation of buildings around the city earlier that day. When members of the Irish Volunteers and the ICA marched up Sackville Street from

---

1 Philip B. Ryan, *The Lost Theatres of Dublin* (Westbury, 1998), p. 174.

THE COLISEUM THEATRE
HENRY ST. & PRINCES ST. DUBLIN

Proprietors: The Coliseum Theatre (Dublin) Ltd.
Managing Director: WILL BLEY
General Manager: GEO. E. MARSH

6.45 MONDAY, APRIL 24TH, 1916 And During the Week **9 O'C.**

ENORMOUS ATTRACTIONS FOR EASTER!

THE TROMBETTAS
CONTINENTAL COMEDY DUO IN THEIR OWN COMPOSITIONS—
1—AVANTI SAVDIA 2—PASTORALE 3—IMITATION

FRED BARNES
THE POPULAR LIGHT COMEDY STAR IN ALL HIS LATEST SONG SUCCESSES

? MY LADY RAG DOLL ?
INTRODUCED BY L. MARTINEK, AS PLAYED BEFORE THE LATE KING EDWARD VII

TOM STUART	MONS. FOOTGERS
DUBLIN'S OWN BURLESQUE IMPRESSIONIST	THE FAMOUS ANGLO-FRENCH ENTERTAINER

JAZON AND MONTGOMERY PRESENT THEIR SINGING AND TERPSICHOREAN NOVELTY

REVUE - LAND
(ANYWHERE FOR EFFECT)

THE BIOSCOPE
ALWAYS INTERESTING

WARSAW BROS.
Presenting "ORPHEUS and PAN"

NO EARLY DOORS! NO BOOKING FEES!

CHILDREN HALF PRICE STALLS AND GRAND CIRCLE FOR FIRST PERFORMANCE ONLY

Entrance Henry Street			Entrance Prince's Street	
BOXES (to hold Four) 15/- and 12/6	STALLS 2/-	GRAND CIRCLE 1/-	PIT 6d	GALLERY 3d

ROYAL HIBERNIAN RE-UNION.

EASTER, 1916.

The Past and Present Students R.H.M.S. present their Compliments to

Mr & Mrs. Cahill

and request the pleasure of _their_ Company at a Social to be held in the Gymnasium, R.H.M.S., on Monday, 24th April, 1916, commencing at 8.30 p.m.

The Coliseum Theatre was not the only Dublin venue that intended to host an event on the evening of 24 April 1916. This is an invitation card for a reunion social in the Royal Hibernian Military School in the Phoenix Park on 24 April 1916; presumably this was cancelled in the light of events elsewhere in the city. The school was within sight of the Magazine Fort in the park that had been attacked early on 24 April. (*Courtesy of Kilmainham Gaol Museum, KMGLM 2015.0308*)

Liberty Hall just after midday, there was not necessarily anything unusual about it; such parades were a regular sight on the streets of many Irish towns and cities. What was unusual was that when the column drew level with the GPO, the Volunteers turned to their left and seized the building.

The outbreak of the Rising took Dublin's citizens and the British authorities by surprise. In truth, it even took some of those who participated in it by surprise. So it is worth taking a brief glance at the newspapers that some of them would have read that morning, to get a sense of the issues that were in the public eye at Easter 1916. In *The Irish Times* the news was dominated by the war: German fears of a British offensive in Ypres, the ongoing Battle of Verdun, lists of the Irish casualties and even a charity rugby match to raise funds for injured soldiers between the 'crocks' of Leinster and the 'crocks' of Ulster. The teams were composed of former internationals (hence the name); the crocks of Ulster won. Inevitably, the annual Easter horse races at Fairyhouse also occupied a good deal of column space, and Yeats' *Cathleen Ní Houlihan* was due to start a run in the Abbey.

The war also shaped the Easter message preached in Christ Church Cathedral by John Bernard, the Anglican Archbishop of Dublin, on Easter

Sunday. He spoke of 'the conquest of evil; the conquest of death ... this is the conviction – the faith that right must conquer might – with which our armies go forth, with which we send them ... The Easter message is a message of victory. But it tells of a victory that always came through tears and blood. So it always is in the crusades of earth, for the disciple is not above his master.'[2] His son had been killed at Gallipoli in 1915.

In the letters page of *The Irish Times*, 'an Irish nationalist' who had spent 'many months at the front in Flanders' suggested that conscription should be extended to Ireland if it applied to England and Scotland – 'Why should Irishmen suffer the indignity of allowing other countries to sacrifice everything for our sakes, while our foolish young men play at soldiers in the streets of our cities and the roads and lanes of our country districts?' This was presumably a swipe at groups like the Volunteers; events over the next few days may have changed this assessment.[3]

With the benefit of hindsight, there are fragments of news that hint at what was to come. The *Irish Independent* carried notices of the cancellation of Volunteer parades, buried amidst reports of a vice-regal tour of Ulster, golf notices, mention of an Austrian offensive and a 'remarkable but honest offer' to get a fitted suit from London at a knock-down price.[4] The *Freeman's Journal* covered many of the same issues as the *Independent*, but carried reports on the capture of a boat with weapons in Kerry, and how 'a stranger, of unknown nationality, was arrested in the vicinity and is detained in custody'; this was presumably Roger Casement. It also reported the recovery of the bodies of three men from Castlemaine Harbour in Kerry, who were apparently wearing 'Sinn Féin badges'. These were the Volunteers who had intended to attempt to communicate with the *Aud*, but who drowned after their car drove off Ballykissane Pier in the dark. Nonetheless, the war

---

2   *The Irish Times*, 24 April 1916.
3   *Ibid.*
4   *Irish Independent*, 24 April 1916.

dominated, with reports of fighting at Verdun, Ypres, the Caucasus and Mesopotamia, amongst other places. Two Redmondite candidates would contest the forthcoming Ossory by-election, the annual 'convention' of the GAA was held in Kilkenny, those seeking to profiteer by adulterating dairy products and other foodstuffs were to face stiffer penalties, and the racing at Fairyhouse was prominent amongst the 'holiday sporting arrangements'.[5]

The Easter Rising was, for most people, a bolt from the blue. Attempts to understand it as it happened were hampered by the absence of news. The publication of the daily newspapers was severely disrupted by the events of Easter Week. As the novelist James Stephens noted, during the week of the Rising Dublin was characterised by (amongst other things) 'a state of tension and expectancy which is mentally more exasperating than any excitement could be. The absence of news is largely responsible for this. We do not know what has happened, what is happening, or what is going to happen, and the reversion to barbarism (for barbarism is largely a lack of news) disturbed us.'[6]

The newspapers had plenty to report when they began to reappear in early May. As for the Coliseum Theatre, it had the misfortune to be located directly behind the GPO; it was destroyed during the Rising and never reopened.

The remains of the interior of the Coliseum Theatre after the Rising. (*Courtesy of the National Library of Ireland*)

---

5 *The Freeman's Journal*, 24 April 1916.
6 James Stephens, *The Insurrection in Dublin* (Gerrards Cross, 1992), p. 62.

18

Proclamation of the Irish Republic

THE MANIFESTO

The document pictured here should need little introduction: the Proclamation of the Irish Republic is *the* iconic text of the Easter Rising. While its authorship is uncertain, and the precise circumstances of its composition remain unclear, more is known about how and where it was physically manufactured.

The Proclamation was printed in Liberty Hall, the headquarters of the ITGWU and ICA on Beresford Place. James Connolly, who had been co-opted by the IRB into joining the plans for a rebellion in January 1916, was based there. From January, Liberty Hall (formerly the Northumberland Hotel) became a focal point for much of the planning and preparation of the Rising, and Patrick Pearse, Tom Clarke and Seán MacDiarmada were all occasional visitors. After the outbreak of the war Liberty Hall was briefly adorned with a banner declaring that 'we serve neither King nor Kaiser but Ireland', and after the Rising *The Irish Times* described it as 'the centre of social anarchy in Ireland, the brain of every riot and disturbance'.[1] Liberty Hall was also where Connolly's newspaper, *The Workers' Republic*, was published. The printer was Christopher Brady, and the compositors were William O'Brien and Michael Molloy, all three of whom were also involved in printing the Proclamation.

It was printed on a Wharfdale hand press, bought by Connolly from

---

1 *1916 Rebellion Handbook* (Belfast, 1998), p. 19.

POBLACHT NA H EIREANN.

THE PROVISIONAL GOVERNMENT
OF THE
IRISH REPUBLIC
TO THE PEOPLE OF IRELAND.

IRISHMEN AND IRISHWOMEN: In the name of God and of the dead generations from which she receives her old tradition of nationhood, Ireland, through us, summons her children to her flag and strikes for her freedom.

Having organised and trained her manhood through her secret revolutionary organisation, the Irish Republican Brotherhood, and through her open military organisations, the Irish Volunteers and the Irish Citizen Army, having patiently perfected her discipline, having resolutely waited for the right moment to reveal itself, she now seizes that moment, and, supported by her exiled children in America and by gallant allies in Europe, but relying in the first on her own strength, she strikes in full confidence of victory.

We declare the right of the people of Ireland to the ownership of Ireland, and to the unfettered control of Irish destinies, to be sovereign and indefeasible. The long usurpation of that right by a foreign people and government has not extinguished the right, nor can it ever be extinguished except by the destruction of the Irish people. In every generation the Irish people have asserted their right to national freedom and sovereignty; six times during the past three hundred years they have asserted it in arms. Standing on that fundamental right and again asserting it in arms in the face of the world, we hereby proclaim the Irish Republic as a Sovereign Independent State, and we pledge our lives and the lives of our comrades-in-arms to the cause of its freedom, of its welfare, and of its exaltation among the nations.

The Irish Republic is entitled to, and hereby claims, the allegiance of every Irishman and Irishwoman. The Republic guarantees religious and civil liberty, equal rights and equal opportunities to all its citizens, and declares its resolve to pursue the happiness and prosperity of the whole nation and of all its parts, cherishing all the children of the nation equally, and oblivious of the differences carefully fostered by an alien government, which have divided a minority from the majority in the past.

Until our arms have brought the opportune moment for the establishment of a permanent National Government, representative of the whole people of Ireland and elected by the suffrages of all her men and women, the Provisional Government, hereby constituted, will administer the civil and military affairs of the Republic in trust for the people.

We place the cause of the Irish Republic under the protection of the Most High God, Whose blessing we invoke upon our arms, and we pray that no one who serves that cause will dishonour it by cowardice, inhumanity, or rapine. In this supreme hour the Irish nation must, by its valour and discipline and by the readiness of its children to sacrifice themselves for the common good, prove itself worthy of the august destiny to which it is called.

Signed on Behalf of the Provisional Government,

THOMAS J. CLARKE.
SEAN Mac DIARMADA.   THOMAS MacDONAGH.
P. H. PEARSE,   EAMONN CEANNT,
JAMES CONNOLLY.   JOSEPH PLUNKETT.

William Henry West, an Englishman who had previously printed James Larkin's paper, *The Irish Worker*. He was tarnished by this association and was forced to move to smaller premises; he sold his press to Connolly as no other printer was likely to produce *The Workers' Republic*. On the morning of 23 April 1916 – Easter Sunday – Connolly and Thomas MacDonagh met Brady, O'Brien and Molloy in Liberty Hall and MacDonagh gave them the text of the Proclamation. Brady stated later that the handwriting was definitely not Connolly's, as 'I was familiar with his scrawl.[2] O'Brien thought that it was Pearse's handwriting, and Pearse seems to have been the most likely author, with possible amendments to the text made by Connolly and MacDonagh (though Éamonn Ceannt was another possibility).[3] Having read through it, Brady, O'Brien and Molloy began to print it, and were protected by armed members of the ICA as they did so (Connolly seems to have intended that if they were captured, they could plead that they had printed it under duress). The paragraphs of the document were set out individually but despite the fact that they had borrowed additional type from West (the original owner of the press), they did not have enough to print the entire document and were forced to improvise: Brady used sealing wax to convert an 'F' into an 'E', and the text was printed in two sections. The British troops who raided Liberty Hall later in the week, on realising that the type had not been taken out of the press, printed copies of the bottom half of the document as souvenirs.

By 1 a.m. on Easter Monday, 2,500 copies of the Proclamation had been printed on poor-quality poster paper obtained in Saggart. Having been proofed by Connolly, they were then passed over to Helena Molony for distribution. Following the taking of the GPO, the Proclamation was

---

2 Christopher Brady, Bureau of Military History (BMH) Witness Statement (WS) 705, p. 5.
3 Liam O'Brien, BMH WS 323, p. 6; NLI MS 5,442: 'The Republican Proclamation of 1916' (paper given to Bibliographical Society of Ireland by Joseph J. Bouch, 25 March 1935).

read aloud by Pearse outside the building and copies were then distributed throughout the city.

The Proclamation declared an Irish Republic to be a 'Sovereign Independent State', in line with Ireland's right to independence. It states that those carrying out the rebellion were simply the latest in a long line of people to assert Irish independence through force of arms, and lists the various organisations involved – Irish Volunteers, ICA and IRB – while acknowledging the aid provided by 'exiled children in America' and 'gallant allies in Europe'. It then moves on to more egalitarian sentiments, in which Connolly's influence is perhaps evident – guarantees of male and female suffrage in the future Republic, equal rights, equal opportunities, civil and religious freedom, a willingness to pursue the prosperity of the nation and all of its parts and, most famously, the promise to cherish 'all the children of the nation equally'. However, the rest of that sentence indicates that this reference to children was metaphorical rather than literal; the new Republic would be 'oblivious of the differences carefully fostered by an alien government, which have divided a minority from the majority in the past'. It is difficult to interpret that as anything other than a veiled reference to unionism (though it should be pointed out that, for a republican document, God was invoked surprisingly often). Finally, and contentiously, the Proclamation ended by stating that until such time as a representative government could be established, the 'Provisional Government' – the IRB's military committee, who were named at the bottom – would take matters into their own hands; a break from the previous Fenian position and one that inadvertently set a questionable precedent.

How seriously were these sentiments taken? The very existence of the Proclamation was unknown to most of the insurgents until it was read out and distributed. In the GPO during the Rising Pearse and Joseph Plunkett were apparently overheard discussing the prospect that a German prince could become a putative Irish monarch should German assistance guarantee the success of the Rising. Clarke, on being asked by Min Ryan of

Cumann na mBan why he and his co-conspirators emphasised a Republic, replied that 'you must have something striking to capture the imagination of the world'.[4]

So was the Proclamation simply rhetoric? It has become commonplace to suggest that its ideals were betrayed in independent Ireland but, as Fearghal McGarry has observed, Catholicism, cultural nationalism, militarism and resentment of British rule were more potent motivations for the rank and file of the Rising than a doctrinaire belief in republicanism. 'The patriarchal, clericalist and conservative state that emerged from Ireland's revolution was perhaps less a betrayal of the Proclamation than a consequence of the fact that its ideals were never deeply rooted within the nationalist movement that won independence.'[5] Yet its rhetorical power was undeniable, as it came to be extensively reprinted: 1,000 copies were printed and distributed in Dublin to mark the first anniversary of the Rising in 1917. These, and subsequent editions, used different fonts: the copy pictured here is one of the rare, and distinctive, originals.

---

4 McGarry, *Rebels*, p. 187
5 Fearghal McGarry, '1916 and Irish Republicanism: Between Myth and History', in John Horne and Edward Madigan (eds), *Towards Commemoration: Ireland in War and Revolution, 1912–1923* (Dublin, 2013), p. 52.

19

Irish Republic Flag

THE OCCUPATION OF THE GPO

During the Easter Rising, two republican flags flew over the GPO. One, made of green poplin, was manufactured on Cork Street at the request of A. P. Reynolds; it was then painted by Theo Fitzgerald (whose impression of the material was that it was actually bunting) in the home of Constance Markievicz on Leinster Road in Rathmines, where it hung on the wall of a back bedroom in the days before the Rising. James Connolly apparently gave it to R. H. Walpole of the ICA; Walpole and Seán O'Hegarty raised it on the flagpole at the south-east corner of the GPO shortly after the building was seized.[1]

The GPO opened on Sackville Street in 1818 as the main Dublin postal office (with a national reach). It was a post office in 1916 and is still, at the time of writing, a post office, albeit with an additional symbolism due to its role in the Easter Rising, when it was the main base of the headquarters garrison. We cannot be entirely certain why the building was chosen for this role, but it was one of the most prominent symbols of state authority on the north side of the Liffey. It also served as a communications hub, a point not lost on the insurgents, though key elements of the communications infrastructure elsewhere in the city were not seized, notably the telephone exchange in Crown Alley and Amiens Street Station, from which news of the outbreak of the Rising was communicated to London. Another

---

1   R. H. Walpole and Theo Fitzgerald, BMH WS 218.

possible reason for the seizure of the GPO is more prosaic: Sackville Street was the widest street in Dublin and had long been a venue for large political gatherings; it was a street on which such activity was sure to be noticed.

At around midday on 24 April, approximately 150 men and women led by Connolly, Patrick Pearse and Tom Clarke marched from Liberty Hall and seized the GPO. Having ejected customers from the public office and staff from the upper offices (which took some time), the insurgents – now known collectively as the 'Army of the Irish Republic' – made their preparations in the building. Windows were smashed to prevent them being shattered by gunfire later and various materials were placed in the empty windows to provide protection to the defenders. Given that the GPO was at the heart of a commercial area, barricades were hastily assembled using whatever material came to hand and supplies were seized from nearby restaurants and shops (with receipts being offered on occasion). Members of the newly ensconced garrison smashed through the walls of neighbouring buildings to create access passages; hospitals and kitchens were also prepared within the building.

Outside, Sackville Street was thronged by curious crowds. Members of the unarmed DMP were withdrawn from the streets due to fears that they would be attacked (not least by members of the ICA who might wish to settle scores left over from 1913). This contributed to a bizarre atmosphere, as law and order broke down and the insurgents had to contend with looters seizing material from both their barricades and the shops in the area.

Some of earliest fighting of the Rising took place near the GPO. Mounted troops – Lancers – were fired on as they came to investigate what was happening on the afternoon of 24 April; the carcass of one of their horses lay in the middle of Sackville Street for the duration of the fighting. The experience of many within the GPO, however, was often one of boredom and uncertainty, with more prosaic concerns such as food

The ruins of the GPO after the Rising, as seen from the Nelson Pillar.
(*Courtesy of Kilmainham Gaol Museum, KMGLM 2015.0089.06*)

taking precedence over fighting in many memoirs. Yet this belies the reality of the situation in which the insurgents found themselves. There was gunfire and sniping in the vicinity of Sackville Street during the first days, but the heavy fighting began in earnest from Wednesday onwards; and by the weekend the GPO over which the flag had flown was a burnt-out hulk; an irony, given that it had only recently re-opened after extensive renovations. It would not become fully operational again until the 1930s.

Numerous people saw the 'Irish Republic' flag that flew over the building during the week. On the night of Tuesday 25 April an impromptu sing-song began in a temperance hall on Burgh Quay; one woman leaving it was heard to remark 'thanks be t' God I lived to see the grand green flag flyin' over the JPO [*sic*]'.[2] By Friday 28 April the same witness recorded seeing the 'white letters of the words "Irish Republic" on its surface gradually scorch a deep brown hue. Now and then it is buried in an upheaval of thousands of fragments of burning paper … during four days and nights it has flown above the building proudly and defiantly; it now begins to hang its head as if in shame. At nine o'clock the General Post Office is reduced to ruins. Its four granite walls look like the bones of a skeleton skull. Its core is nothing

---

2 Mick O'Farrell, *1916: What the People Saw* (Cork, 2013), p. 232.

The Irish Republic flag displayed by troops at the Parnell Monument after the Rising.
It has been hung upside down: a traditional statement of victory.
(*Courtesy of Kilmainham Gaol Museum, KMGLM 2015.0452*)

---

but smouldering debris. The fluttering of the flag grows feebler. In the dimness of the night I see it give an occasional flicker, as if revived by the gust of air. At length at 9.51 p.m. the staff supporting it begins to waver, and in a second falls out towards the street.'³

It was perhaps appropriate that the flag tipped over that evening, as Friday 28 April was the day that the GPO was finally abandoned by its garrison. There can be no doubting the iconic status of the flag flown over the GPO as a symbol of an insurrection. The point was not lost on those members of the Royal Irish Regiment who later posed with it at the Parnell monument, having captured it and turned it upside down as a 'Regimental Trophy'.⁴

---

3   *Ibid.*, pp. 245–6.
4   R. H. Walpole and Theo Fitzgerald, BMH WS 218.

20

Irish War News

THE FIRST DAYS OF THE RISING

Joseph Stanley was a printer in Dublin. Originally from Drogheda, he had been involved in publishing a number of small militant nationalist newspapers, such as *The Spark,* but his printing press was smashed in a raid a few weeks before the Rising. On Easter Monday he was summoned to the GPO for a meeting with James Connolly and Patrick Pearse, who sounded him out about producing impromptu propaganda bulletins. To that end, Stanley and a number of others occupied O'Keeffe's printworks on Halston Street.[1]

The *Irish War News*, dated Tuesday 25 April, was the first and most substantial of the publications that they produced there. It is a curious text: the first three pages were presumably prepared in advance and were apparently written by Pearse. The first page was a commentary on a recent article in the *New Statesman* that had attempted to paint a picture of what England would be like under German rule. The author of the *Irish War News* felt that this had inadvertently painted an accurate picture of Ireland under English rule (the article's emphasis on how education would be used as a tool of German indoctrination may well have caught Pearse's attention). This was followed by a highly dubious article claiming that 'British subsidised scandal-mongering' about the affairs of King Leopold

---

1 Military Archives, Dublin: Military Service (1916–1923) Pensions Collection (MSPC): MSP34REF20034 (Joseph Michael Stanley).

IRISH WAR NEWS

THE IRISH REPUBLIC.

Vol. 1. No. 1. DUBLIN, TUESDAY, APRIL 25, 1916. One Penny

"IF THE GERMANS CONQUERED ENGLAND."

In the London "New Statesman" for April 1st, an article is published—"If the Germans Conquered England," which has the appearance of a very clever piece of satire written by an Irishman. The writer draws a picture of England under German rule, almost every detail of which exactly fits the case of Ireland at the present day. Some of the sentences are so exquisitely appropriate that it is impossible to believe that the writer had not Ireland in his mind when he wrote them. For instance :—

"England would be constantly irritated by the lofty moral utterances of German statesmen who would assert—quite sincerely, no doubt—that England was free, freer indeed than she had ever been before. Prussian freedom, they would explain, was the only real freedom, and therefore England was free. They would point to the flourishing railways and farms and colleges. They would possibly point to the contingent of M.P.'s, which was permitted, in spite of its deplorable disorderliness, to sit in a permanent minority in the Reichstag. And not only would the Englishman have to listen to a constant flow of speeches of this sort ; he would find a respectable official Press secretly bought over by the Government to say the same kind of things over and over, day after day of the week. He would find, too, that his children were coming home from school with new ideas of history. . . They would ask him if it was true that until the Germans came England had been an unruly country, constantly engaged in civil war. . . . The object of every schoolbook would be to make the English child grow up in the notion that the history of his country was a thing to forget, and that the one bright spot in it was the fact that it had been conquered by cultured Germany."

"If there was a revolt, German statesmen would deliver grave speeches about "disloyalty," "ingratitude," "reckless agitators who would ruin their country's prosperity. . . . Prussian soldiers would be encamped in every barracks—the English conscripts having been sent out of the country to be trained in Germany, or to fight the Chinese—in order to come to the aid of German morality, should English sedition come to blows with it."

"England would be exhorted to abandon her own genius in order to imitate the genius of her conquerors, to forget her own history for a larger history, to give up her own language for a "universal" language—in other words, to destroy her household gods one by one, and put in their place of Belgium had been part of a campaign to seize Belgium's colonial possessions in Africa and that figures who had been assailed for their willingness to defend Belgian rule in the Congo by 'hired ink-slingers', such as Arthur Conan Doyle and E. D. Morel, were now being held up as a witness to German atrocities. There was, unsurprisingly, no mention of Roger Casement, who had confirmed allegations of atrocities committed by the Belgian regime in the Congo.

Various digs at Home Rulers followed, but the final page ('stop press') pointed out that the *Irish War News* was printed that day:

> … because a momentous thing has happened. The Irish Republic has been declared in Dublin … The Irish troops hold the City Hall and dominate the Castle. Attacks were immediately commenced by the British forces and were everywhere repulsed. At the moment of writing this report (9.30 a.m., Tuesday) the Republican forces hold all their positions and the British forces have nowhere broken through. There has been heavy and continuous fighting for nearly 24 hours, the casualties of the enemy being much more numerous than those on the Republican side. The Republican forces everywhere are fighting with splendid gallantry. The populace of Dublin are plainly with the Republic, and the officers and men are everywhere cheered as they march through the streets.

Most of these claims were open to challenge. There had not, as yet, been heavy fighting on the streets. That would come later in the week. City Hall had been seized on Easter Monday, but the small ICA garrison there had surrendered by Tuesday morning. It was the case, however, that with the exception of City Hall, the republican forces in Dublin still held the positions they had seized the previous day: the areas around the GPO and behind the Four Courts north of the Liffey, and around Boland's Bakery, St Stephen's Green, City Hall and the South Dublin Union, all south of the river. There was a logic to the seizure of some of these. The area around the

Four Courts, for example, overlooking the quays and close to Broadstone Station, could serve as an obstacle to the arrival of reinforcements coming into the city. The fact that the same preparations took place in different locations – the smashing of windows, the stockpiling of water, the seizure of multiple buildings to act as outposts – shows that some training had taken place before the outbreak of the Rising, and that some thought had gone into how the insurgents might actually fight. The relatively small number of insurgents were, however, stretched thinly across the city.

The intensity of the fighting varied across these different areas as the week wore on, but on the whole it would intensify. Tuesday 25 April was also the day on which martial law was declared in response to the outbreak of what the authorities termed the 'Sinn Féin rebellion'. While some troops had been rushed to Dublin as early as Monday evening, by Wednesday they began to arrive in Dublin in large numbers, as the British sought to crush the rebellion in earnest.

Although the outbreak of the Rising prompted a communications breakdown throughout the city (and outlandish rumours of German landings, for instance, were rife), the publication of the *Irish War News* shows that the need for propaganda by word as well as deed had not been lost on the rebel leadership – irrespective of the reality of the events unfolding.

21

Homemade Bomb

Desperate Measures

This crude device is a homemade grenade; one of many made in various locations before and during the Rising. Its existence points to a perennial problem faced by the Irish Volunteers: while they could certainly train themselves, conduct drills and even obtain customised uniforms, obtaining weapons was another matter. In March 1916 the British authorities estimated that the Volunteers had no more than 5,291 firearms: British, German and Italian rifles, along with shotguns, revolvers and pistols. Even before the abortive mission of the *Aud*, the Volunteers had been trying to augment their meagre arsenal: service rifles were occasionally bought from deserters or stolen from troops (military regulations that forbade the carrying of weapons into pubs were sometimes exploited, as helpful teenagers would offer to mind rifles for thirsty troops who would emerge to find their weapons gone). Different brigades had varying levels of success in these attempts, but if it was difficult to obtain firearms, it was virtually impossible to obtain heavier weapons. Necessity being the mother of invention, the Volunteers began to make such weapons, and in one location had an unlikely workforce to do so.

It is unclear where this improvised grenade was manufactured, but there are at least three possibilities: Liberty Hall, St Enda's or Larkfield, a former mill in Kimmage owned by the wealthy Plunkett family. Larkfield's expansive grounds and proximity to the Dublin mountains meant that it was used as a focal point for Volunteer drilling and exercises. By early 1916 it had also become a home for perhaps as many as ninety men. Irish

Joe Good (*left*) photographed with John 'Blimey' O'Connor and Ernie Nunan, before the Rising. (*Courtesy of Kilmainham Gaol Museum, KMGLM 2012.0107*)

Volunteer groups had been organised in Irish communities in Scotland and England, and from late 1915 these British-born Volunteers – first, second and third generation immigrants from nationalist backgrounds – began to travel back to Ireland (in some cases to avoid the prospect of conscription). The old mill buildings at Larkfield were used to house the newly arrived 'British' Volunteers. These men had come from London, Liverpool, Manchester and Glasgow; many of the Glaswegian contingent had moved to Dublin in early 1916 after a number of raids on collieries to steal explosives (some of which seem to have made their way to Dublin) had forced them to go on the run.

Encamped at Larkfield in secure but basic conditions, they drilled, trained and began to make munitions – ammunition, lances and explosive devices – using explosives stolen from a quarry near Tallaght, and cans and lengths of pipe. There were enough tradesmen within their ranks to equip them with the necessary skill sets and according to the London-born Volunteer Joe Good, who helped to make such weapons at Larkfield, they were 'crude hand grenades [made] out of 2" x 4" [inches] cast iron down-pipe, with a flange end through which a long bolt passed. A small hole penetrated one of the flanges, through which the fuse was inserted.'[1] It is unclear where the bomb in the picture was made, as similar activities took place in St Enda's. Obviously it was either never used or didn't work.

---

1   Joe Good, *Inside the GPO 1916: a First-hand Account* (Dublin, 2015), p. 40.

The so-called 'Kimmage Garrison' departed Larkfield laden down with such weapons on the morning of 24 April 1916. Considering the distance to their destination, it made sense that, when they got to Harold's Cross, over fifty of them decided to get on a tram. In a striking display of probity, Joseph Plunkett's brother, George, insisted on buying the necessary tickets, and they dismounted at O'Connell Bridge. Despite the fact that many of the Kimmage Garrison were ignorant of the geography of Dublin (an unfamiliar city to most of them), its members were active in central positions such as the GPO throughout the week. This meant that, just as the British suppression of the Rising was often conducted by Irish-born troops, at least some of those who fought in the rebellion, the stated purpose of which was to end British rule in Ireland, had been born in Britain. The irony went both ways, and is best exemplified by the experience of John McGallogly,

a Glaswegian Volunteer, who later found himself debating the merits or otherwise of the Rising with his guards while in captivity in Richmond Barracks: 'I ventured a remark and one of the guards, a red-haired Irishman, said, "You shut up you Scotch bastard. You only came over here to make trouble."'[2]

A recruitment advertisement for the Irish Volunteers from 1916. Note how many of their companies held their manoeuvres at Larkfield.
(Courtesy of the Allen Library, Christian Brothers, Dublin)

---

2 John McGallogly, BMH WS 244, p. 12.

22

A Cricket Bat that Died for Ireland

LOOTING AND STREET-FIGHTING

In April 1916 this cricket bat was on display in the window of a sporting goods store: J. W. Elvery & Co. at 46–47 Lower Sackville Street, on the same side as the GPO. On being donated to the National Museum in 1981, it was dubbed 'the cricket bat that died for Ireland'.[1]

It was 'killed' by a British .303 round that is still lodged in the bat, probably fired in the early days of Easter Week, before Sackville Street was bombarded and became an inferno. What is less clear is how the cricket bat made its way out of Elvery's. Presumably it received a helping hand, for when the Rising broke out on Easter Monday, shops on Sackville Street were being looted within a matter of hours.

Sackville Street was one of Dublin's commercial heartlands, but it was also surrounded by vast areas of slums. Dublin in 1913 had a higher proportion of its population living in slums than any other city in the United Kingdom and this was still the case in 1916. When the DMP were withdrawn from the streets on the first day of the Rising, according to *The Irish Times* 'the underworld of the city quickly realised their opportunity, and first tackled the shops on Lower Sackville Street', which is where Elvery's was located (unlike many of its neighbours on the street, Elvery's survived the Rising). Children featured prominently in this looting;

---

1 Brenda Malone, 'The Cricket Bat that Died for Ireland: Objects from the Historical Collections of the National Museum of Ireland' (http://thecricketbatthatdiedforireland.com).

and in a poignant human detail, one of the first shops to be looted was Noblett's sweet shop at the corner of North Earl Street. It did not end there; soon, 'boys and girls were swaggering about, dressed in the most fantastic apparel, and all had their arms full of mechanical and other toys, hockey and golf sticks, and all kinds of articles used in popular pastimes'.[2] Perhaps a cricket bat was amongst them?

There were few provisions stores near Sackville Street that could provide basic necessities to Dublin's tenement dwellers. Many of the goods looted were items from high-end department stores that the urban poor could never normally afford. Poverty took precedence over politics. As the looting continued, women from the slums seemed to join the children, and a bewildering variety of goods were taken: clothing, drink, footwear (which was a prime target), jewellery, sweets, tobacco and even fireworks, which were set off in the middle of Sackville Street on Tuesday afternoon.

Many of the Volunteers observed this in disgust, and some fired over the heads of looters. In fact, Pearse apparently stated that looters should be shot, but was unwilling to back this up with action. While occasionally Catholic priests sought to stop the looting, the British Army did little to prevent it; indeed, some troops were involved in looting themselves, much to the consternation of the military authorities. The looting was inevitably curtailed as the fighting intensified later in the week, but this presented different difficulties for local businesses. A number of department stores, such as Arnott's and the Henry Street Warehouse (later Roches Stores), reopened on 5 May, and by 6 May the Henry Street Warehouse was advertising 'costumes and coats injured by rifle fire'.[3] Evidently, the cricket bat from Elvery's was not the only piece of merchandise to have put its life on the line for Ireland in 1916.

---

2 *1916 Rebellion Handbook*, p. 5.
3 Stephanie Rains, *Commodity Culture and Social Class in Dublin 1850–1916* (Dublin, 2010), p. 206.

23

Memorial Cup awarded for the Defence of Trinity College, Dublin

A LOYAL GARRISON

It may seem unusual that the insurgents did not target Trinity College, Dublin, one of the most imposing complexes in Dublin city centre. However, given the small numbers who participated in the Rising, and considering the composition of much of Trinity's staff and student body, it is perhaps understandable. It was highly unlikely that a rebellion in pursuit of Irish independence would have received a universally warm welcome in Ireland's oldest and most prestigious university.

According to *The Irish Times*, during the Rising Trinity College proved 'true to its traditions'.[1] In political terms, the college was strongly unionist in composition (one of its sitting MPs was, after all, the unionist leader Edward Carson). In 1915 its waspish provost, John Pentland Mahaffy, had blocked 'a man called Pearse' from addressing the college's Gaelic Society just after the outbreak of the First World War (Pearse's penchant for anti-recruiting speeches was presumably a factor), and 471 staff and students of the college were killed in the war.[2]

When the Rising broke out on 24 April, Arthur Luce, a fellow of the college, home on sick leave from the Western Front, walked up Sackville Street and brought word back to the college of what was happening. The

---

1 *1916 Rebellion Handbook*, p. 15.
2 J. V. Luce, *Trinity College Dublin: the First 400 Years* (Dublin, 1992), pp. 129–31.

chief steward, Joseph Marshall, ordered the college porters to secure the gates and to invite any passing soldiers in. Marshall armed them with old pikes that had been captured during the Fenian rebellion of 1867, and, as a former member of the DMP, he himself was armed with 'my old historic revolver and my Tipperary blackthorn, which I brought into use in the wild riots in Dublin in September 1913'.[3]

Trinity also had its own Officer Training Corps (OTC), though many were away for Easter. Westland Row station was quite close to the OTC armoury, which was deemed vulnerable to attack, but by nightfall the college had perhaps forty-four defenders, including members of the Australian and New Zealand Army Corps (ANZAC) and South African troops. These troops were either on leave or, like Luce, were on sick leave; some had been fired upon while in uniform on the streets. One of the ANZACs was Michael McHugh of Queensland, who had seen action in Gallipoli before being evacuated with influenza and enteric fever in September 1915. He was walking past Trinity when a porter armed with a pike successfully implored him to help defend the college.

Trinity's erstwhile defenders were concentrated in and around Parliament (Front) Square on the campus. Many of the imperial troops who found themselves in Trinity took up firing positions on the roofs overlooking College Green, from where one of them shot dead the twenty-year-old republican messenger Gerald Keogh as he cycled past the college early on Tuesday 25 April. Keogh was presumably the 'Sinn Féiner' brought into the Provost's House, whose body was left in a room for a number of days before it was briefly buried in the Provost's garden some days later (Arthur Griffith's small Sinn Féin party was almost immediately, and incorrectly, blamed for the outbreak of the Rising). The central location of the campus heightened fears that it would be attacked, but the British

---

3 Georgina Fitzpatrick, *Trinity College Dublin and Irish Society, 1914–1922: a Selection of Documents* (Dublin, 1992), p. 11.

Badges of the TCD Officer Training Corps.
(*Courtesy of the Glasnevin Trust*)

authorities decided to use it as a base for that very reason. Members of the Leinster Regiment arrived from the Curragh Camp, Co. Kildare, on Tuesday and were welcomed into the college. On Wednesday 26 April troops began to arrive on campus in much larger numbers; an emergency hospital was established in house 15, as Parliament Square filled with troops and the paraphernalia of war, including artillery and cavalry. Trinity hosted perhaps 4,000 troops in total, and at least two soldiers killed in the fighting were also buried temporarily on the campus.

It should be noted that a handful of intrepid undergraduates arrived to sit exams during the week in which Dublin went to war. Written exams went ahead on Tuesday 25 April amidst the sound of gunfire; oral exams took place on Wednesday 26 April before being suspended as the serious fighting commenced.

On a practical note, the occupation of Trinity blocked communications between the Irish garrisons in the GPO and on St Stephen's Green. It also seemed to dissuade looting in the vicinity, a fact not lost on local business owners. A committee of businessmen based in Grafton Street and College Green was established after the Rising, and raised £700 to pay for a number of memorial cups, including the one pictured here. They were presented in a ceremony on 5 August 1916 in the Provost's Garden on campus. The original was given to the commander of the OTC and was valued at £50, weighing 170 ounces. Replicas were given to the other members, and to some of the soldiers who had also helped to defend the college. Not everyone received one, but amongst those deemed worthy of a memorial cup was the ANZAC Michael McHugh, who had returned to his unit on the Western Front. On learning that he was due to receive it, McHugh requested that the adjutant of the OTC write to his commanding officer stating that McHugh's presence in Dublin at the award ceremony – and far away from the firing line – was expressly requested. It seems that he failed to get to the ceremony, but he still received the cup, presumably by post. Having survived the war, McHugh returned to Australia in April 1919.

The front gate of Trinity College guarded by troops.
(*Courtesy of the heirs of T. W. Murphy*)

A temporary grave in Trinity. (*Courtesy of Mick O'Farrell*)

24

Wesley Hanna's Account of the Rising

A Civilian Perspective

Wesley Hanna was from Limerick and worked as an accountant in Switzers department store on Grafton Street. His family home was in Limerick, so he seems to have been a regular commuter to Dublin. On Tuesday 25 April he arrived in Dublin's Kingsbridge (now Heuston) Station, to be confronted with an unexpected scene; the station was occupied by the military and he had to pass through two lines of soldiers with fixed bayonets to leave. As he did so, 'we looked round in wonderment – quay at Guinness side held by fixed bayonets'.[1] Having soon learned what was happening: that 'S.F.' (Sinn Féin) was in possession of various sites in the city and that looting had taken place on Sackville Street, Hanna managed to make his way over to Ballsbridge, stopping to watch troops march along Morehampton Road. Encountering fighting in Ballsbridge, where 'a fairly smart fusillade was in progress', he was forced to make a diversion along the River Dodder (he subsequently included a map in his account of the Rising, pictured here, of what he described as a 'hot spot' of fighting in Ballsbridge).

Indeed, Hanna described coming close to the fighting on a number of occasions, so much so that he felt he could 'write a book with what

---

1   All quotations and details in this chapter are taken from 'Letter from Wesley Hanna to his family, 2 July 1916', *Letters of 1916* (http://dh.tcd.ie/letters1916/diyhistory/items/show/345).

25 OAKLANDS PARK,
BALLSBRIDGE,
DUBLIN.

may remember that the road branches there thus:—

[sketch map: Ball's bridge / Elliott's + / Pembroke Road / Lansdowne Rd / To Victor's and into town / Haddington road / Beggar's Bush Bks]

The house at the corner ◀ was held by the S.F. party with a machine gun and the soldiers were at Ball's bridge, so you can imagine what a hot spot it was for 3 days until 14 dead S.F. rebels were accounted for and the house taken. The house farther on marked × at the corner of Haddington Road is — rather was — a death trap and some of Victor's volunteer corps were shot point on Monday — one killed out

I've seen'. He describes the noises of the guns going off in his vicinity – 'a new gun that goes off like a motorbike exhaust – pop – pop – pop' and a machine gun 'like a glorified Electric bell without the gong'. On one occasion the fighting came a little close to home when British soldiers opened fire on a rebel in the vicinity who had shot at one of their number: 'the place was alive with firing all round for quite 10 minutes – then the end – they got him dead!' When a bullet hit Hanna's neighbour's house he 'skipped you may be sure double quick time'. Hanna also mentioned how he and a 'chum' had cycled up into the Wicklow Mountains 'with field glasses to see if we could distinguish the damaged area of the city'.

Hanna's account, written in the aftermath of the Rising, was detailed and humane; he readily admitted his ignorance of much of what had gone on but was perhaps too hard-headed to fall prey to the rumours that swept Dublin during Easter Week in 1916. However, he did record that Roger Casement had been shot on the Easter Sunday and that Hanna Sheehy-Skeffington had been taken prisoner and reported that she would be shot too. The ordeal of the civilians caught up in the fighting was also a cause for concern. For instance, he remarks that 'the food question has become acute' and he also records the experience of people like Mrs D. Smith, whose house was hit by fire 'sending splinters flying, some through her hair'.

The letter was written on paper stamped '25 Oaklands Park, Ballsbridge, Dublin'; presumably, this was an address he had stayed at in Dublin, though on the first page '25' had been crossed out and replaced with '27'. Hanna was not without a sense of humour: as he observed and heard of events in what is now Dublin 4, he noted that 'if it weren't so awfully tragic it would be amusing to see the swells round here carrying home bread'. His lucid and vivid testimony seems to have been intended for members of his family; at the top of the first page he had written a number of names, with the exhortation 'pass round please quickly'.

In the immediate aftermath of the Rising, innumerable witnesses to what had happened on the streets of the Irish capital during the Easter

Rising wrote letters akin to Hanna's. However, it was not until the 1940s that the Irish government established the Bureau of Military History to collect testimonies from veterans of the independence movement. This archive was released in 2003. The Bureau's understandable emphasis on the testimonies of participants should not obscure the value of the testimonies of non-participant witnesses, such as Hanna, who stood outside the barricades. As for Hanna himself, he signed off his account of the Easter Rising with the jaunty assurance that he was 'still smiling'. He eventually became the company secretary of Switzers, a post he held until his retirement in the 1960s.

Wesley Hanna
(*Courtesy of Michael Hanna*)

25

Watercolour Sketch of a Barricade at the Shelbourne Hotel

THE BRITISH RESPONSE

This sketch by the Dublin-born stained-glass artist Michael Healy (a contemporary of the more famous Harry Clarke) depicts figures at a barricade composed of vehicles outside the Shelbourne Hotel on St Stephen's Green, in Dublin's south inner-city on Easter Monday, 24 April. The Green was seized by members of the ICA that afternoon, and was the venue for fighting from an early stage.

At the eventual inquiry into what had happened in Dublin – some of which was conducted, coincidentally, in the Shelbourne Hotel itself – the Lord Lieutenant, Ivor Churchill Guest, Viscount Wimborne, claimed that 'ever since the departure of the Irish Divisions for the front I had been of the opinion that the Irish garrison was quite inadequate'. In other words, the garrison in Ireland had been eroded by the requirements of the Western Front. Both Wimborne and Chief Secretary Augustine Birrell claimed (possibly in an attempt to deflect criticism) to have been worried that 'we have not enough troops in Ireland in case of internal trouble'. The War Office apparently had opposed the idea of sending an additional division to Ireland, as this would have put a gap of a fortnight in the training and dispatch of troops to the Western Front.[1]

---

1 *Royal Commission on the Rebellion in Ireland: Report of Commission* (London, 1916), pp. 34–5.

There is a kernel of truth behind Wimborne and Birrell's claim, as in April 1916 the garrison in Dublin was relatively small (and was weakened even further as most of it had Easter Monday off). However, troops from other bases in Ireland such as the Curragh began to arrive into the city as early as Monday night. As these troops reached the city and awaited more substantial reinforcements, they began to cordon off the areas seized by the insurgents.

One of the first areas to be dealt with was St Stephen's Green. The Green was originally laid out in the 1660s, but had been reopened in 1880 having been renovated by the Guinness family. Members of the ICA led by Michael Mallin, a weaver and former British Army veteran, seized it on Easter Monday. The majority of the ICA – perhaps in the region of 100 – were here and observers were struck by the youth of those involved. One of the two police constables killed on the first day of the Rising, Michael Lahiff, was shot outside the Unitarian church on the Green (allegedly by Constance Markievicz).

Why was the Green seized? It dominated a large tract of the southeast inner-city, with plentiful supplies to be had in the hotels and shops nearby. Perhaps more significantly, it was a major transport hub and its seizure would allow the ICA to disrupt the movement of troops in this area of the city, at least in principle.

Trenches were dug in the park, probably at the main gates and near Dawson Street (though the precise location is unclear). Food was seized and barricades were built in the vicinity; cushions were even taken from the gate lodge to make at least one of the trenches more comfortable. Vehicles were also commandeered, and there was outrage when a civilian was shot dead while trying to retrieve his cart from a barricade near the Shelbourne Hotel, which, as a major Dublin landmark, featured prominently in accounts of what happened. Perhaps the barricade in the image here was the one in question?

Unfortunately for Mallin and his followers, the Shelbourne Hotel also provided a vantage point from which to command the Green. Troops were dispatched to the Green from Dublin Castle and arrived there around 4 a.m. on Tuesday. They began to fire down into the trenches in the park just after dawn and forced the ICA to retreat to the Royal College of Surgeons on the west side of the Green by 8 a.m., passing the statue of the Green's benefactor, Arthur Edward Guinness, Lord Ardilaun, as they did so. The occupation of St Stephen's Green lasted no more than a few hours.

The British military authorities imposed severe restrictions on movement in some parts of Dublin during and after the Rising. This improvised pass was issued at Kingstown (Dún Laoghaire) to permit its bearer – a Lieutenant Mitchell – to pass through the military lines. (*Courtesy of Glasnevin Trust*)

The Royal College of Surgeons is one of a number of Dublin buildings to still bear battle scars from the Easter Rising on its exterior; the marks of small arms fire are clearly visible on the upper storeys of the building facing the Green. As for the interior, at one point during the occupation Mallin reprimanded a young ICA member for damaging a portrait of Queen Victoria. However, as British attention shifted elsewhere once the

Green was evacuated, fighting eased off until the surrender on Sunday and the area survived relatively unscathed. Another set of bullet marks can be seen on the north-eastern side of Fusiliers' Arch (the memorial to members of the eponymous unit killed in the Boer War), which sits on the corner of the Green, across from the college. These were presumably caused by British troops firing at the college from their vantage point in the Shelbourne Hotel.

Pocket watch belonging to Michael Mallin, awarded for service in the British Army.
(*Courtesy of Kilmainham Gaol Museum, KMGLM 2015.0306*)

26

Certificate of Service for the 16th (Irish) Division, 27 April 1916

THE EASTER RISING AND THE GREAT WAR

During the week in which the Easter Rising took place, the 16th (Irish) Division experienced its first major engagement at Hulluch on the Western Front. At 5 a.m. on 27 April they were bombarded by German artillery, which was followed by an attack with chlorine gas. Trench fighting followed and was repulsed. There were further gas attacks that day and on 29 April. The 16th Division lost 538 dead in the attacks of 27 and 29 April, 183 of whom were members of the 8th Battalion of the Royal Dublin Fusiliers; the unit of which Sergeant J. H. Mason, the recipient of this certificate, was a member. To put it another way, in the week of 24–29 April 1916 there were more Irish people killed at Hulluch than in Dublin. This certificate is a small reminder of the wider context within which the Easter Rising must be understood.

This reality was not lost on those who participated in the Rising: how could it be? The night before Seán Heuston's execution, in a letter to his sister, he touched upon how he and his colleagues might be judged for their actions: 'Let there be no talk of foolish enterprise. I have no vain regrets. Think of the thousands of Irishmen who fell fighting under another flag at the Dardanelles.'[1] Thousands of Heuston's contemporaries, from both

---

1   Piaras F. MacLochlainn, *Last Words: Letters and Statements of the Leaders Executed after the Rising at Easter 1916* (Dublin, 1990), pp. 110–11.

The Irish Brigade

No 21230 Sgt. J.H. Mason
8th R. Dublin Fus.

I HAVE READ WITH MUCH PLEASURE THE REPORTS OF YOUR REGIMENTAL COMMANDER AND BRIGADE COMMANDER REGARDING YOUR GALLANT CONDUCT AND DEVOTION TO DUTY IN THE FIELD ON April 27th 1916 AND HAVE ORDERED YOUR NAME AND DEED TO BE ENTERED IN THE RECORD OF THE IRISH DIVISION.

W.B. Hickie
Major-General,
Commanding 16th Irish Division.

Dublin and the rest of Ireland, were killed or wounded when the 10th (Irish) Division landed at Gallipoli the year before. The Irish losses at Gallipoli had left a sufficiently sore mark that when the British authorities sought a military governor to suppress the Rising, they decided against their first choice, General Ian Hamilton, because of his association with the Dardanelles campaign.

Undermining the patriotic assumption that Hill 16 in Dublin's Croke Park was created out of the rubble of the Easter Rising is a very different reality: the terrace existed before the All-Ireland finals of 1915 and received its original name after an attempt to capture the eponymous hill in Gallipoli in which the Connaught Rangers had suffered significant casualties.

Perhaps as many as 210,000 Irishmen enlisted in the British Army alone during the First World War, and around 35,000 of them were killed; numbers that dwarf the events of the Rising. Many Irish troops in the British Army were involved in suppressing the Rising. While the 8th Battalion of the Royal Dublin Fusiliers suffered losses at Hulluch, some of its reserve battalions – the 4th, 5th and 10th – saw action on the streets of Dublin.

Yet the Rising cannot be understood as anything but part of the war. The separatist republicans who planned and executed the Rising did so within the context of a war that gave them both an opportunity to strike and a prospective ally (Germany). The British suppressed it in the manner in which they did precisely because they were at war themselves and feared such German involvement. Irish responses to 1916 were often (though not always) hostile, especially – and understandably – on the part of the families of serving troops. The perception that the Rising was pro-German goes a long way towards explaining that hostility; in the aftermath of the Rising, some republicans conceded that their British captors had actually protected them from angry crowds of Dubliners. The context of the war also accounts for some of the British tactics in the Rising, such as the obdurate insistence on frontal assaults at places such as Northumberland Road and the use of artillery.

The events of 1916 in Dublin were noted further afield. As reported in the Austro-Hungarian Empire, the Rising was linked to on-going war propaganda about the 'small nations' that Britain supposedly sought to defend. The French were concerned about the implications of 1916 at a time when the Battle of Verdun was taking a horrific toll on their army; they suspected that the Germans were capitalising on British fears of a German expeditionary force to Ireland to distract the British from their obligations on the continent. Ambivalence and hostility towards the Rising was also recorded amongst Irish troops on the Western Front, but when their German opponents sought to exploit this they received a stout rebuff. In May 1916 some enterprising German soldiers on the Western Front erected a notice saying 'Irishmen! Heavy uproar in Ireland: English guns are firing at your wifes [sic] and children!'[2] Under cover of darkness, a soldier of the Royal Munster Fusiliers, who had also been part of the 16th Division – Francis Biggane from Cork – stole it as a trophy. He was killed at Passchendaele the following year.

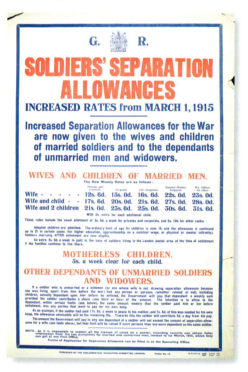

A notice of separation allowances from 1915. The families of serving troops were particularly hostile to those who fought in the Rising, for understandable reasons.
(*Courtesy of the National Library of Ireland*)

---

2 Cormac Ó Comhraí, *Ireland and the First World War: a Photographic History* (Cork, 2014), p. 172.

27

Compensation Claim for Damage to 73 and 73a Lower Mount Street

The Ambush at Mount Street Bridge

This is one of the standard forms on which property owners who suffered damage or losses during the Rising could apply for compensation. In this case, the applicant was George Cathcart Hemphill of 11 Ely Place, who was also applying on behalf of his co-trustees: William Webb, currently on military service, and William Atkins, who lived in Canada. The properties in question were 73 and 73a Lower Mount Street, consisting of 'houses and premises'. The 'premises' was the Merrion Temperance Hotel at No. 73, at the junction of Lower Mount Street and Grattan Street; the 'houses' were presumably the tenements next door. The repairs required at No. 73 indicate the nature of the damage: the main issue was to replace windows at the front and back, and to repair damage to the interior walls and the roof. It is impossible to be certain what caused this, but given the nature of the repairs, it seems the damage may have been done by gunfire coming through the windows and hitting the interior walls.

This is a reasonable supposition, as some of the heaviest and bloodiest fighting of the Rising took place a few hundred yards south of these buildings, around Mount Street Bridge and Northumberland Road. These streets were within the large and diverse region in the south-east of the city that was to have been held by the 3rd Battalion, under the command of a teacher, Éamon de Valera, who established his headquarters in Boland's Bakery beside the Grand Canal. This area included the road and rail links

Property Losses (Ireland) Committee, 1916.

51 ST. STEPHEN'S GREEN, EAST, DUBLIN.

Claim for Damages caused during the Disturbances on the 24th April, 1916, and following days.

I Charles George Cathcart Hemphill now residing at 11 Ely Place in the City of Dublin do both on behalf of myself and my Co-Trustee Lieutenant Marshall William Treherne Webb (who is on Military Service now residing abroad) and William Howard Atkins (who resides in the County of in Canada) do hereby solemnly and sincerely declare that on or about the 26th day of April 1916, damage was done to the undermentioned Property, namely :—* Houses and premises known as 73 and 73A Lower Mount Street Dublin and such damage was occasioned to the best of my belief by** housebreaking and looting by Looters during the said disturbances and also occasioned by the occupation of the said premises by the Military during the said disturbances

And I further declare that the Property and Articles specified on the other side were so destroyed or damaged; ~~that the Cost Price of same was as shown in each case; that at the time of the destruction or damage they were respectively of the Values specified under the head "Value of Property at time of Destruction or Damage"~~; and that, in consequence of such destruction or damage, claim is hereby made for the sums specified under the head "Amount Claimed"; that the Claim is made by me as one of the persons entitled to the Lessees interest under the within mentioned lease ; and that no person is interested in the said property, except ‡ myself said Co-Trustee Marshall William Treherne Webb and my so far as I know co-owner William Howard Atkins (who are the other persons entitled to the said lessees interest) and our Landlady Mrs E. M. Brady and our tenant Thomas Murty O'Beirne

and that it is not insured by me or any other person, § except as follows, namely:— by me and my Co-Trustee on behalf of themselves and the said William Howard Atkins in the County Fire Office Company, Policy No. 263183, Amount £ 1650-0-0 against damage by fire or lightning

" , " , " , £
" , " , " , £

And I make this solemn Declaration conscientiously believing the same to be true, and by virtue of the provisions of the Statutory Declarations Act, 1835.

Made and subscribed the 7th day of August 1916, at 110 Grafton St in the said City, County, before me, a Justice of the Peace for the said City County.

Signature of Claimant: C. G. C. Hemphill

Louis H Brindley
J.P. City of Dublin

NOTE—This Claim is to be furnished in duplicate, and should be accompanied by the Policies of Fire Insurance and the last receipt, in each case, or certified copies of same. When completed it is to be forwarded to the Secretary of the Committee, 51 St. Stephen's Green, East, Dublin.

to the ferry port at Kingstown, which was an obvious landing point for any reinforcements that might be sent to Dublin by ship. Should these reinforcements march directly into the city centre, they were probably going to come along Northumberland Road and cross Mount Street Bridge. There they could be ambushed, and this is precisely what happened.

A small number of Volunteers, led by Michael Malone, seized a number of buildings: Clanwilliam House on the northern side of the canal and, on the southern side, a schoolhouse on Northumberland Road and a private residence, No. 25, across the street. On 26 April members of the 178th Infantry Brigade arrived at Kingstown. They split into two groups as they entered the city: one went via Donnybrook; the other, comprising the 7th and 8th Battalions of the Sherwood Foresters, was instructed to continue directly on to Trinity College and went via Northumberland Road. As the latter group did so, Malone and his men opened fire on them in the confined space of a suburban street. Given that the troops had been mobilised rapidly and sent to Dublin from Watford via Liverpool, they had left most of their heavier weapons behind. They were ambushed at 3.25 p.m., were ordered to continue on into the city irrespective of the cost at 5.30 p.m., and only began to get the upper hand when reinforcements

Members of the 3rd Battalion of the Irish Volunteers being led away to captivity after surrendering. Under the command of Éamon de Valera, they had occupied buildings in the south-east of the city, including Boland's Bakery. (*Courtesy of Mercier Archive*)

with grenades and machine guns began to arrive at 8 p.m. In all, 220 soldiers and officers were killed or wounded in a prolonged, intense and bloody encounter – approximately half of all the British military casualties of the Rising. There were also casualties amongst the Volunteers who had ambushed them, including Malone, who was briefly buried in the garden of 25 Northumberland Road.

That night the Sherwood Foresters were sent to Ballsbridge, having been relieved by the South Staffordshire Regiment. The compensation form for 73 and 73a Lower Mount Street claimed the damage to the properties was done 'on or about' 26 April, which links it to the fighting that took place that day. Given that the buildings lay some distance away from Mount Street Bridge itself, any damage inflicted by troops was probably done as they continued on in the direction of Trinity College over the next few days. If the damage was caused by gunfire from troops, they may have been firing at looters (according to the claim, some of the damage was caused by looting). Or, equally, British troops may have taken the precaution of firing into the building lest there be a repeat of what happened on Northumberland Road.

Michael Malone, who commanded the Volunteers in 25 Northumberland Road. He was killed in the building. His brother Willie, a sergeant in the Royal Dublin Fusiliers, had been killed the previous year at the second Battle of Ypres.
(*Courtesy of Mercier Archive*)

28

Fianna Hat belonging to Seán Healy

Death of a Boy Soldier

Seán Healy was a member of Na Fianna Éireann, the republican youth organisation originally founded by Bulmer Hobson and Constance Markievicz in 1909. Na Fianna had a militarist and nationalistic ethos from its inception and had been deliberately conceived of as a counterweight to the imperialist ethos of Robert Baden-Powell's Boy Scouts, but in terms of its activities, Na Fianna was a mirror image of the Scouts. Many of its members graduated into the ranks of the Irish Volunteers after its foundation in 1913: two of the men executed after the Rising, Con Colbert and Seán Heuston, had first come to prominence in Na Fianna. They tended to be involved in many of the same activities as the Volunteers – Na Fianna had been prominent in the Howth gun-running – so it was perhaps inevitable that members of the organisation fought, and were killed, in the Easter Rising. Healy was one of them, and this hat was part of his Fianna uniform.

Healy was born in 1901 and lived at 188 Phibsborough Road, Dublin. He was an apprentice plumber, following after his father, with whom he had been moving weapons around on Easter Sunday. Healy was never mobilised, but like many others he attempted to get involved in the Rising once it had started. He reported to Thomas MacDonagh's garrison at the Jacob's biscuit factory on Tuesday 25 April and was given a message to take to the Volunteers in Phibsborough – presumably MacDonagh felt that as a local, Healy would be able to deliver it. As he made his way to

his destination he briefly stopped off at his house and asked his mother for some money to buy cigarettes. A few minutes after he left, he received an horrific head wound at the corner of the Phibsborough Road and the North Circular Road. He was taken around the corner to the Mater Hospital, where he died two days later, on Thursday 27 April. The cause of death may have been shellfire. He was buried in Glasnevin Cemetery.

Perhaps as many as thirty children under the age of sixteen, including three members of Na Fianna, were killed in the Easter Rising. Healy was just fourteen years old when he was killed.

Senior officers of Na Fianna Éireann, c. 1913–14. Seated, left to right: Paddy Holohan, Michael Lonergan, Con Colbert. Standing, left to right: Garry Holohan, Pádraig Ó Riain.
(*Courtesy of Eamon Murphy*)

29

Royal Irish Constabulary Carbine from the Battle of Ashbourne

The Rising in Meath and Co. Dublin

Ashbourne is in Co. Meath and was the scene of one of the few successful engagements of the Easter Rising that took place outside Dublin, when members of the Irish Volunteers led by Thomas Ashe and Richard Mulcahy defeated a substantial number of RIC officers in a five-hour gun battle. Joseph Lawless of the Fingal Battalion of the Irish Volunteers captured this rifle at Ashbourne; it is a standard RIC carbine, short and light for mobility, and very different to the weapons the Volunteers had.

The Fingal Battalion – officially the 5th Battalion of the Dublin Brigade – had assembled at Knocksedan near Swords in north Co. Dublin on Easter Monday under the leadership of Thomas Ashe. Originally from the Kerry Gaeltacht, Ashe worked as a teacher in Lusk and was active (and prominent) in a wide range of nationalist organisations before 1916: the Gaelic League, the GAA, the IRB and, of course, the Irish Volunteers. There were perhaps sixty active Volunteers assembled in north Co. Dublin on Easter Monday. This group included just half of those who had turned up for manoeuvres the previous day, Easter Sunday. Their numbers were further reduced after Ashe was requested to dispatch reinforcements to the GPO; he sent around twenty of his men into Dublin city in response to this request.

The overall purpose of Ashe and the men under his command was to distract the military from the city and, if need be, to disrupt transport

links that might be used to bring reinforcements into Dublin. There were also vague hopes that they might eventually link up with the Volunteers in the north inner-city, around the Four Courts. As befitted their origins in farming communities, the Fingal Volunteers had shotguns and a small number of Howth Mausers. Most were on bicycles, though Ashe himself, in a vaguely dashing touch, apparently had a motorbike.

On Easter Monday the Volunteers attempted to blow up the Great Northern Railway's line into Dublin at Rogerstown. On Tuesday they were joined by Richard Mulcahy, a member of the 2nd Battalion of the Dublin Brigade, who had been unable to join his colleagues (they ended up occupying Jacob's biscuit factory). On Wednesday they attacked a number of RIC barracks and commandeered a bread van; on Thursday they stayed at Borranstown. Then, on Friday, they set out for Batterstown, with the aim of disrupting the Midland Great Western Railway, the main line from Galway, which ran into Broadstone Station near Phibsborough. The Volunteers passed through Ashbourne along the way, realising as they did so that the local RIC barracks was occupied. They took up positions along the roadside before noon and exchanged gunfire with the constables inside for about thirty minutes before the latter surrendered.

At this point a convoy of seventeen cars carrying fifty-five RIC constables, led by County Inspector Alexander Grey, passed through the village, possibly en route to Slane. Seeing what was happening, they disembarked and prepared to attack the Volunteers. Mulcahy took some of the Volunteers to outflank the newly arrived RIC officers and a five-hour gun battle ensued. The RIC surrendered only after their most senior remaining officer, District Inspector Harry Smyth, was killed (Grey had been injured early in the day; he died from his injuries some weeks later). Eight members of the RIC were killed at Ashbourne, as were two Volunteers.

The engagement at Ashbourne was a rare triumph for the Volunteers. Ironically, apart from Smyth, every participant on both sides was Irish; it could be classed, perhaps, as a civil war in microcosm.

When the order to surrender came through to Ashe's men two days later, on Sunday 30 April, they were encamped at Kilsallaghan. Before surrendering, one of the Volunteers, Joseph Lawless, decided to hide one of the RIC carbines taken at Ashbourne and wrapped it in a cement bag to hide it under a thorn bush in a field. Lawless was an avid photographer and had brought a small Kodak camera with him; he took photographs of the aftermath of the engagement at Ashbourne. He hid the camera and some of his other personal effects nearby, before returning to his colleagues to surrender to the authorities. Lawless was subsequently interned in Frongoch in Wales, but on going to retrieve his possessions after his release from captivity a few months later, he found that the camera was gone and the only photos of the ambush at Ashbourne along with it. He was able to retrieve the carbine and later donated it to the National Museum; the camera may have been a less risky prize for its discoverer than the rifle that was left behind.

30

A Globe belonging to Liam Mellows
The Rising in East Galway

This globe is, perhaps, an appropriate object with which to take note of Liam Mellows. Having been born in Lancashire, Mellows was brought up in Wexford, made his name in Galway and ended up in America after 1916. Mellows had been a national organiser for Na Fianna and the Irish Volunteers, and in March 1915 he had been appointed to organise the Volunteers in Galway. In 1916 he oversaw one of the few instances of militant activity outside Dublin during the week of the Rising. It took place in east Co. Galway, a region with a long tradition of agrarian insurgency that was alive and well in 1916, and which co-existed, sometimes uneasily, with the politics of militant nationalism and republicanism.

While Galway city and its major towns were staunchly Redmondite (violent clashes with republicans were not unknown), the rural areas around Athenry, Kinvara and Clarinbridge were strongly separatist in sentiment. On Easter Monday Larry Lardner, the commander of the Galway Brigade, and Tom Kenny, a blacksmith from Craughwell who was active in the IRB and GAA, mobilised perhaps 500 men from Oranmore, Clarinbridge, Athenry, Newcastle and Derrydonnell. Mellows, who had previously been exiled to Staffordshire, only made contact with the Galway Volunteers on Monday night. To some degree, more militant nationalism in Galway built upon traditions of agrarian unrest and resentment at landlords and 'ranchers'; certainly, the Volunteers in Galway were drawn from the ranks of small farmers, artisans and labourers, and Kenny, who was more radical

on social issues than figures like Mellows, was involved in agrarian insurgency.

On Tuesday 25 April RIC barracks in Clarinbridge and Oranmore were attacked unsuccessfully by the Galway Volunteers. Athenry, where local Volunteers were already tearing up railtracks, cutting telegraph wires, preparing food and making weapons, then became their focal point.

The Galway Volunteers were poorly armed, with shotguns and a handful of rifles; they were to have been armed with weapons landed from the *Aud*, but without them, what could they really do? There was also uncertainty about what they were supposed to do in any case, but the fact that the Volunteers had come out in east Galway, along with the cutting of rail and telegraph links, caused panic in Galway city itself. One consequence was the creation of an impromptu citizens' militia (drawn in part from the Redmondite National Volunteers) to help the authorities maintain law and order in the city. Members of the Irish Volunteers were arrested, while the National Volunteers also assisted the RIC in Craughwell and Loughrea. On Wednesday morning an RIC patrol accompanied by members of the National Volunteers was ambushed near Galway city and an RIC constable, Patrick Whelan, was shot dead.

By Thursday, however, as British reinforcements arrived in Galway city and county, it became apparent that the Galway Volunteers had no clear idea of what they might do next. A warship in Galway bay fired shells at the area around Athenry, prompting the Volunteers to retreat

Liam Mellows
(*Courtesy of Mercier Archive*)

south to Moyode Castle, thence to Lime Park and finally to Tulira Castle. There seemed to be little point in sustaining the effort, so on Friday 200 of the insurgents returned home. Although Mellows had insisted that the Volunteers should stand their ground, instead they disbanded on the advice of a local priest, who apprised them of what had happened in Dublin.

The Galway press was vociferous in its condemnation of the Volunteers and 328 Galway men were detained in Frongoch internment camp after the Rising. As for Mellows, he escaped to America but later returned; he was executed on the orders of the Free State government during the Civil War in December 1922.

31

James Connolly's Blood-stained Shirt
A Wounded Visionary

During the week of the Rising James Connolly was wounded in the shoulder and leg near the GPO, and evidence of the damage to his shoulder can be seen in the bloodstain on this undershirt, which he was wearing at the time. It is even the subject of a poem by the Scottish poet Sorley MacLean, entitled 'Ard mhusaeum na h-Éireann/The National Museum of Ireland' – surely few shirts have been eulogised thus.

The man who wore it was – is – one of the public faces of the Rising, comparable in that regard only to Patrick Pearse. Connolly was born in Edinburgh to Irish émigré parents. In his youth he worked in a variety of labouring jobs and also served in the King's Liverpool Regiment. Working as a manure carter in Edinburgh (the same job as his father), Connolly got involved in trade unionism and became a committed socialist. He had a gift for organising, not to mention publicity and propaganda. He moved to Ireland in 1896, where he was involved in labour politics, insofar as they existed at the time, and established the Irish Socialist Republican Party. Connolly had a varied career as a trade union organiser and propagandist in Ireland and also, for some years, in America, where he was involved from an early stage in Big Bill Haywood's Industrial Workers of the World (the IWW, or 'Wobblies'). He returned to Ireland in 1910 and joined James Larkin's ITGWU, becoming its Ulster organiser, based in Belfast, before moving to Dublin and taking a leading role in the 1913 Lockout.

What was a man like Connolly, who possessed a strong sense of social justice and a firm commitment to the emancipation of the working class and the overthrow of capitalism, doing in the GPO in 1916? Was his socialism compatible with Irish nationalism and republicanism? Connolly was an original thinker as well as a publicist, an autodidact who provided an influential left-wing analysis of Irish conditions in works such as *Labour in Irish History*, but who also displayed a willingness to change his views according to conditions. The Home Rule crisis and outbreak of the First World War forced him into a more nationalistic position, in which the struggle for a social revolution became intertwined with the struggle against British capitalism and imperialism. In January 1916 he was co-opted by the IRB into co-operating with their rebellion because of his position as the leader of the ICA. The ICA's inclination towards rebellion and its alarming tendency to draw attention to itself by activities such as mock attacks on the gate of Dublin Castle caught the eye of Tom Clarke and Seán MacDiarmada, who feared that Connolly might inadvertently trigger a British crackdown by such actions.

Connolly essentially acted as the military commander at the GPO during the Rising, but was gravely wounded; while his leg wound ensured that he could not walk (he was famously executed while sitting on a chair), he also developed gangrene in the shoulder wound that stained the shirt. His death may have been a foregone conclusion, even before he was shot.

Connolly was not without flaws – his political commitments may have caused him to neglect his family, and he could be rash and intemperate on occasion. Yet he possessed a deep and genuine sense of social justice beyond his socialism. For Connolly, independence without the emancipation of the poorest and most degraded in Irish society was a contradiction in terms. Had he not become involved in the Rising, Connolly may have become a footnote to Irish history, a curious but marginal agitator in a country that tended not to welcome revolutionary socialists. Bulmer Hobson of the IRB left this caustic assessment of Connolly:

His conversation was full of clichés derived from the earlier days of the socialist movement in Europe. He told me that the working class was always revolutionary, that Ireland was a powder magazine and that what was necessary was for someone to apply the match. I replied that if he must talk in metaphors, Ireland was a wet bog and the match would fall into a puddle. I thought of this later as I watched the Dublin mob, not joining Connolly in the Post Office but looting the shops in O'Connell [Sackville] Street.[1]

Caustic it may be, but Hobson's recollection sums up both Connolly's ambitions and the obstacles that he faced. His involvement in the Rising, as testified to by this item of clothing, means that Connolly is today remembered as a hero of the Irish revolution.

James Connolly
(*private collection*)

1   McGarry, *Rebels*, p. 178.

32

Artefacts from the *Helga*

A Mistaken Impression

Many accounts and testimonies from the Easter Rising refer to the *Helga*, a gunboat that came up the River Liffey and is generally credited with having devastated much of Dublin city centre with artillery. Yet the *Helga*'s role in the suppression of the Rising illustrates the degree to which appearances can deceive.

That there was indeed a vessel called the *Helga* – these artefacts are proof of that – and that it did come up the Liffey during the week of the Rising is not in dispute. Nor is the fact that the ship was equipped with guns, although it is stretching matters too far to describe it, as even *The Irish Times* did, as a gunboat.

The *Helga II* was actually built in Dublin in 1908 for the Department of Agriculture and Technical Instruction. She was designed to be a research vessel complete with laboratories; the first notable task of her varied career was to take part in the pioneering Clare Island Survey conducted in 1909–11, a study of virtually every aspect of the eponymous island off the coast of Co. Mayo. In 1915 the ship was requisitioned by the Admiralty for anti-submarine activity, based in Kingstown (Dún Laoghaire) and equipped with two guns: a twelve-pound gun at the front and a three-pound gun at the rear.

On Tuesday 25 April the *Helga* made her way up the River Liffey and fired at Boland's Bakery. The shells missed, but as a precaution the commandant at Boland's, Éamon de Valera, had a tricolour flag placed on the roof of a nearby distillery to serve as a diversion. On Wednesday 26 April the ship moved further up the river to attack Liberty Hall, but its progress was halted by the cast-iron Loop Line railway bridge, which also blocked the *Helga*'s view of Liberty Hall. Matters were complicated by the presence of a Guinness steamer at Butt Bridge and instead of firing directly at the building, the crew of the *Helga* – two of whom apparently refused to operate the guns – were forced to lob shells over the bridge to drop

them onto Liberty Hall. They began shooting at 8 a.m., and fired perhaps twenty-four shells before retiring. Liberty Hall remained relatively intact.

These events do not tally with the image of a gunboat laying waste to Dublin city centre that is often presented in accounts of the Rising. Some members of the GPO garrison were convinced that the shelling of their position that commenced on Wednesday had come from the *Helga* and it is not impossible that shells from the *Helga* could have reached the GPO. However, field artillery – eighteen-pound guns that were more powerful than the weapons on the *Helga* – were dispatched to Dublin from Athlone on Monday, and they would have done far more damage, although most of the destruction on Sackville Street arose from fires breaking out, rather than from the impact of the shelling itself.

Volunteer Joe Good, a member of the GPO garrison, recalled British soldiers pulling up paving stones in D'Olier Street for gun trails: long sections of metal fixed into the ground to lessen the recoil of artillery pieces. Once this was done, an artillery piece began to fire at the building he was in ('Kelly's Fort') at the corner of Bachelor's Walk and Sackville Street. On the other side of the GPO, Sergeant Major Samuel Lomas of the Sherwood Foresters recorded that an eighteen-pound gun was fired from the end of Moore Street.

It was perhaps understandable that the relatively modest weapons of the *Helga* would be blamed for devastating Dublin, given that it would have been in a more visible location – the Liffey – than some of the artillery located elsewhere. It may also have been the case that facts were not going to stand in the way of a good story – so the *Helga* remains an integral part of the folklore of the Rising.

After the founding of the Irish Free State the *Helga* was renamed the *Muirchu* (*Seahound*) and remained in service until after the Second World War. She was on her way to Dublin to be broken up when she sank off the Tuskar Rock on 8 May 1947.

The *Helga*. Note the guns mounted at the bow and stern of the ship.
(*Courtesy of Mercier Archive*)

Flag from the *Helga*.
(*Courtesy of the National Museum of Ireland*)

33

Rubble and Cartridges from the GPO
A Souvenir of Sackville Street

The fires that engulfed Sackville Street during the Rising destroyed the GPO and only the outer façade survived (what exists today is effectively a reconstruction). This mass of metal and debris was fused together by the ferocity of the blaze that engulfed the interior of the building after the roof was ignited by shells and collapsed. The fire damage may also have been intensified by the homemade bombs that the Volunteers had hoped to use, many of which were stored in the basement of the building and which, according to Joe Good, blew up after the Volunteers had abandoned the building.[1] By the end of the week the façade of the building chosen as the headquarters of the Easter Rising was one of the few structures left standing on the western side of Sackville Street.

Yet the eventual destruction of Sackville Street belies the strange atmosphere that pervaded it at the start of the Rising. A recurring theme in many testimonies, both from combatants and other eyewitnesses, was the presence of curious crowds of onlookers on the street in the first days of the Rising. To a certain degree, the outbreak of the Rising was an opportunity for some and an extraordinary spectacle for many others, as groups of curious civilians gathered to observe the proceedings around Sackville Street even amidst the sporadic gunfire that could be heard in the vicinity (it should be said that many of them stayed well back).

---

1   Good, *Inside the GPO*, p. 106.

Life went on in the city in some surprising ways. Good, for example, related how in the early days of the week he had stumbled into a pub on Abbey Street to find some of the clientele drinking at the bar, and was advised by one of them to watch out for 'them military on Capel St'.[2] Even as late as Tuesday night, groups of people were reported to be walking around Sackville Street as if nothing out of the ordinary had happened. Yet another crowd of onlookers gathered on Sackville Street at 9 a.m. on Wednesday – during a lull in the bombardment – but were scattered when a machine gun began to fire down Westmoreland Street at around 10 a.m.; by that afternoon, Sackville Street was described as 'a veritable "no-mans land".'[3]

Curiosity about what was happening may have been giving way to a burgeoning awareness that these events were potentially of great significance. James Stephens, who chronicled the atmosphere of rumour and uncertainty that pervaded the city, claimed that at least some Dubliners had a grudging regard – 'almost a feeling of gratitude' – for the tenacity of the Volunteers by the Wednesday of Easter Week, 'for if they had been beaten the first or second day the city would have been humiliated to the soul'.[4] While curious onlookers may have been driven from the streets by Wednesday, some inhabitants of the city remained on the streets in a more active capacity. Volunteer Oscar Traynor recorded an old man scooping up pieces of shrapnel when the British bombardment began on Wednesday: 'I asked him what he was doing and what he intended to do with the stuff. He said, "Souvenirs".'[5] Whoever collected the fragment of debris from the GPO pictured here – and more were collected – may have been thinking along similar lines.

---

2   Ibid., p. 72.
3   O'Farrell, *1916: What the People Saw*, p. 235.
4   Stephens, *The Insurrection in Dublin*, p. 39.
5   McGarry, *Rebels*, p. 226.

Michael O'Rahilly's car. 'The O'Rahilly' had been involved in attempts to call off the Volunteer mobilisation after the sinking of the *Aud*, but decided to participate when the Rising finally broke out. His De Dion Bouton car, in which he travelled into Dublin city centre on Easter Monday, was used in a barricade on Prince's Street, beside the GPO. (*Courtesy of Mercier Archive*)

British soldiers and civilians in the ruins of Henry Street in Dublin following the 1916 Rising. (*Courtesy of Mercier Archive*)

34

Handkerchief embroidered in Marrowbone Lane, 30 April 1916

The Fighting in South-west Dublin

By way of contrast with what was happening in other parts of the city as the Rising was inexorably crushed, the conditions in Jameson's Distillery in Marrowbone Lane seem to have been sufficiently relaxed to permit one of the small garrison there to embroider this handkerchief on 30 April.

Members of F Company of the 4th Battalion occupied the distillery while most of their colleagues, led by Éamonn Ceannt, occupied part of the vast complex of the South Dublin Union. This was Ireland's largest workhouse, with 3,200 inmates on a sprawling fifty-acre site on the current location of St James's Hospital. Perhaps 120 members of the Volunteers (including Cathal Brugha) assembled on Emerald Square on 24 April before moving down Cork Street to seize the union and a number of other buildings in the vicinity. The location of the South Dublin Union may have been chosen to block the movement of troops from Richmond Barracks in Inchicore, the Royal Hospital at Kilmainham and possibly Kingsbridge Station, where reinforcements from the Curragh would disembark (no attempt, however, was made to seize the station itself). The South Dublin Union was one of the few areas of the city (along with North King Street) in which heavy fighting took place at extremely close quarters; much of the combat elsewhere in Dublin during the Rising took the form of sniping from longer ranges. There was heavy fighting in the complex on Monday, Tuesday and Thursday as some of the union buildings were occupied by British troops, but again,

Apr 30 1916
During the siege of
Marrowbone Lane

their attention shifted elsewhere as the week went on and the Volunteers in the South Dublin Union surrendered only on Sunday 30 April.

Other buildings in the area were also seized: Watkins Brewery in Ardee Street was held by Volunteers under the Limerick Fianna and Volunteer leader Con Colbert (who was later executed); Jameson's Distillery on Marrowbone Lane and Roe's Distillery in Mount Brown were seized as well. According to Bob Holland, who was in Marrowbone Lane, before the Rising Colbert 'never spoke about anything else unless it was connected with Irish history and all his lectures centered [sic] around the subject of "Why we failed". His answer to this question was always "Drink and want of discipline and loose talk."'[1] It was ironic then that Colbert and many of those under him ended up occupying distilleries (though none of the Volunteers in these premises availed of their wares).

As the week wore on Colbert and the other outliers decided to relocate to Marrowbone Lane, as it had more supplies and the other sites that had originally been seized were too far away from the South Dublin Union. Perhaps 145 people were present in Marrowbone Lane over the course of the week, including a detachment from Cumann na mBan (some of whom had been at a Gaelic League ceilí with Volunteers on Easter Sunday), but they were largely relegated to the roles of cooks and couriers. Some, however, were recruited to help the Volunteer snipers.

Marrowbone Lane was the scene of heavy, if intermittent, fighting on the Wednesday, Thursday and Friday of Easter Week. Again, this took the form of sniping from both sides and the Volunteer garrison resorted to making homemade grenades. Colbert also insisted on the preparation of crude pikes, and some enterprising members of the Fianna sneaked out to retrieve weapons from the bodies of soldiers who had been killed. Given the proximity to the Liberties, hungry Volunteers engaged in some impromptu cattle rustling by diverting three heifers being driven down

---

1 Robert Holland, BMH WS 280, p. 12.

Marrowbone Lane into the distillery. Holland was an apprentice butcher and was given the task of converting them into meals, though he apparently got none of the meat himself. He did record, however, that 'Colbert was very anxious about the hide and he asked me a lot about curing it to make mocassins [*sic*].'[2]

Being relatively isolated, rumours of victory and aid were rife, but the reality was that Marrowbone Lane was not a priority for the British, who had withdrawn from the vicinity on Saturday 29 April. There was little or no communication with the other insurgent forces in the city and when the surrender order arrived on Sunday 30 April it prompted anguish and disappointment as the cold reality of defeat set in. The order had taken nearly twenty-four hours to reach Marrowbone Lane – time enough, it would seem, for a handkerchief to be embroidered.

The Guinness Maltstore on Robert Street, which was occupied by troops in response to the seizure of buildings in the district by the Volunteers. The occupation of the complex by troops from a variety of units caused considerable confusion; two employees of the brewery and two officers were shot dead in what appear to have been cases of mistaken identity. Sergeant Robert Flood of the Royal Dublin Fusiliers was acquitted of murder for his involvement in two of the killings. A number of Guinness employees were dismissed by the company for their involvement in the Rising.
(*Courtesy of Diageo Ireland*)

---

2   *Ibid.*, p. 30.

35

A Fragment of a Wall from 16 Moore Street inscribed by Thomas Clarke

SURRENDER

By 3 p.m. on Friday 28 April the roof of the GPO had been hit by shells and quickly caught fire. At around 8 p.m. the garrison within the building (whose numbers had swollen to perhaps as many as 400 during the course of the week) decided to abandon it. It seems that they intended to head through the north inner city to the imposing Williams and Woods factory on King's Inn Street; probably the most substantial remaining building in the vicinity of the GPO. The obvious way of getting there was via Moore Street.

The first group to leave the GPO was led by Michael O'Rahilly, who, despite being involved in attempts to call off the planned mobilisation of the Volunteers the previous Sunday, joined the fighting anyway, quipping that as he helped to wind the clock he would come to hear it strike. As 'The O'Rahilly' and his men charged up Moore Street they were cut down by British troops who had formed a cordon at the far end of the street.

The subsequent evacuation of the GPO was haphazard and disorganised, as members of the garrison left by the side door of the post office and dashed across Henry Street to Moore Lane and Henry Place. They began to break into the houses on Moore Street; a young girl was killed after a Volunteer shot through a door. One Volunteer, James Kavanagh, later recalled, 'I felt very sorry for the people who lived in these houses. By going into them we were bringing death and destruction to the inhabitants ... Seamus

British proclamation dated 30 April 1916; as the decision to surrender had been taken the previous day, this had already been overtaken by events. (*Courtesy of Kilmainham Gaol Museum, KMGLM 2015.0311*)

Donegan, an ambulance man and one of the Liverpool crowd, told me that a girl in a room he was in was struck by a bullet. In the dark he was groping about to find out what was wrong with her. He thought he put his fingers into her mouth, he thought he felt her teeth, but when he struck a match he found that it was through a hole in her skull he had put his finger.'[1] Other civilians were killed on Moore Street itself by gunfire from the soldiers at the end of the street.

The Volunteers were tired and lacked food and water, but some of them began to smash through the walls of the houses to open up access along the length of the terrace. They were hoping to find an escape route, but it soon became obvious they were trapped. In one of the houses decades of the rosaries were recited, though when Michael Collins came across the exhausted Joe Good sitting with his head in his hands he crankily exclaimed, 'Are you [fucking] praying too'?[2] Tom Clarke, James Connolly, Seán MacDiarmada, Patrick Pearse and Joseph Plunkett were all present in Moore Street and eventually,

---

1 McGarry, *Rebels*, pp. 241–2.
2 *Ibid.*, p. 244.

realising the hopelessness of their situation, the decision was taken to surrender. Elizabeth O'Farrell, a midwife who had originally joined Cumann na mBan but had been attached to the ICA as a nurse, clearly stated that the private discussions that preceded the surrender took place in 16 Moore Street, which was owned by a poulterer, Patrick Plunkett, and in which she and number of others attended to wounded rebels, including Connolly. The presence of Connolly seems to have ensured that the room in which he lay came to be used for what O'Farrell described as 'a council of war'.[3] O'Farrell was brought to the various garrisons around the city by a British escort to deliver the surrender orders signed by Connolly and Pearse.

This fragment of wall, inscribed by Clarke, comes from 16 Moore Street. Clarke was devastated by the decision to surrender. According to one Volunteer, Seán McGarry, Clarke 'deplored the fact that the burning of the buildings had deprived us of a glorious fight, in which he felt that even with our limited resources we could give as good as we got'.[4] Moore Street offered a far less dramatic ending, though some of the Volunteers had expected, and intended, to keep fighting.

Clarke was one of the first of the leaders to be executed after the Rising, having told his wife, Kathleen, that his greatest fear was the prospect of being imprisoned once again. He was reported to have initially refused to leave the burning GPO, and was intent on making a stand there (MacDiarmada may have talked him out of this). Had the Volunteers held out for longer in Moore Street, however, he may have met his end there, in combat, as at 12.30 p.m. on 29 April British forces had started breaking into the terraces held by the insurgents in Moore Street, before being informed of the decision to surrender at around 2 p.m.

---

3 'Miss Elizabeth O'Farrell's Story of the Surrender', *Catholic Bulletin*, vii (1917), p. 266.
4 McGarry, *Rebels*, p. 235.

36

A Book damaged by Gunfire from Marsh's Library

Collateral Damage

Some of the more unexpected victims of the Easter Rising reside on the shelves of Marsh's Library, in St Patrick's Close in Dublin. It has the distinction of being the first public library in Ireland, having been established by Narcissus Marsh, the Church of Ireland Bishop of Dublin, at the beginning of the eighteenth century. Two centuries after Marsh's death, troops were located beside the library that bore his name, in St Patrick's Park, which ensured that Marsh's Library lay between them, the Volunteer positions in Jacob's biscuit factory on Bishop Street and the DMP Station on Kevin Street. The area was relatively quiet and free of fighting, but according to the library's minutes, 'on the morning of Sunday 30 April a machine-gun was inadvertently turned on the library from St Patrick's Park'.[1] Several books and some of the internal woodwork were damaged. The book pictured here, through which a bullet has passed, is *Traite de L'Eglise, par Jean Mestrezat, Ministre du Saint Euangile* (published in 1649). The first librarian of Marsh's Library, Elias Bouhéreau, was a French Huguenot – a Protestant who had fled religious persecution – and this had been part of his original collection.

It is unclear when or why Marsh's Library was machine-gunned; it may well have been an accident, or may have been the action of a nervous or

---

1   Marsh's Library: Visitation Minute Book (1707–1924).

TRAITÉ
DE
L'EGLISE,

PAR
IEAN MESTREZAT
Ministre du saint Euangile.

A Geneue.
Et se vend à Charenton:
Par LOVIS VENDOSME, demeurant à
en la Gallerie des Oyseaux, à la C
& au Sacrifice d'Abraham.

M. DC. XLIX.

zealous soldier who feared that 'Sinn Féiners' had occupied the library. This could hardly have been the case, as most of the library staff would have been staunchly unionist in their politics (and a number of them had enlisted in the British Army). The fact that the machine-gunning of the books was recorded as having happened 'inadvertently' was either the truth, or reflected a willingness to give the army the benefit of the doubt.

The books on the shelves were not the only casualties. Apparently the library had sent nearly forty holdings (including a 1590 tome with the eye-catching title *That the Pope is Antichrist*) to be repaired in Thoms on Abbey Street and they were destroyed by the fires that devastated the area around Sackville Street. As the keeper of the library, Rev. Newport J. D. White, observed when writing to the Property Losses Committee in July 1916, 'the value of these things to a library such as this is not to be gauged by what the man in the street would sell them for. Still, I had the man in the street in my mind when I claimed only £16 for the damage done to this library. I did not mention the irreparable injury done to a beautiful oak door rent in 6 or 7 places by large bullet holes.'[2] Perhaps he should have mentioned it; after all, the library received the £16 compensation.

White submitted a slightly different claim for compensation to the military authorities relating to Trinity College, where he was a lecturer in divinity and Hebrew, with rooms looking out onto College Green. Consequently he was instructed to leave the doors open 'for military purposes', which meant, in practice, that two officers of the South Staffordshire Regiment slept there, and White found that a bucket, coal, a clothes brush, towels, dusters and possibly blankets and pillows had gone missing. As with his willingness to accept that his library had been machine-gunned by accident, he was unwilling to blame the officers for his missing possessions. He had 'no complaint to make of their behaviour' and, presumably, gave them the benefit of the doubt.

---

2 National Archives of Ireland: Property Losses (Ireland) Committee Papers, Newport White correspondence: 2928 (3 June 1916), 1192 (21 July 1916).

37

Dublin Fire Brigade Helmet
The Destruction of Dublin

Dublin has had a fire brigade since 1862. This helmet, made of brass, is what they would have worn in 1916 and was the standard model helmet used by the Dublin Fire Brigade from the 1860s to the 1930s. The men of Dublin Fire Brigade are perhaps the unsung heroes of the Easter Rising. They were called out to deal with fires as early as 3.58 p.m. on Monday 24 April, when a fire started by the Volunteers was reported in the Magazine Fort in the Phoenix Park; two more fires, arising from looting on Sackville Street, were also reported on the first day.

In what would turn out to be the busiest week in the fire brigade's history to that point, much of their work also involved rescuing the casualties of the fighting and in this they were aided by members of the St John Ambulance and Voluntary Aid Detachments. In the early days of the Rising, for example, the ambulance logbook of Tara Street fire station records its units transporting wounded civilians to hospital and wounded troops to barracks, as well as collecting the dead; they ranged across much of the city as they did so. As the week wore on it became physically difficult to move through the city and the British military also restricted movement. Those units that were not impeded by the military were often forced to abandon tackling blazes, lest they be caught in crossfire. This meant that it was impossible to deal with many of the calls the brigade received; 'did not attend' appeared in the Tara Street logbook with increasing frequency as the week wore on.[1]

---

1 Dublin City Archives: Tara Street Fire Station ambulance log-book, 24–29 April 1916

Members of Dublin Fire Brigade in an unspecified building after the Rising. Note the helmets. (*Courtesy of the National Library of Ireland*)

By the end of the week Sackville Street was an inferno; just as there was a great deal of material to loot in its shops, so too there was a great amount of material to burn. The British artillery bombardment ignited a barricade across from the GPO, which may have contained reams of paper from the *Irish Times*' reserve printing office on Lower Abbey Street. From there the fire spread to Hoyte's City of Dublin Drug Hall on 17 Lower Sackville Street; its inflammable contents would have helped the fire spread around Abbey Street and the east side of Sackville Street. From the GPO, Oscar Traynor recalled 'the extraordinary experience of seeing the huge plate-glass windows of Clery's stores run molten into the channel from the terrific heat'.[2] In the circumstances, the fire brigade was powerless to tackle a blaze of such ferocity.

(http://issuu.com/dublincitylibrariesandarchive/docs/dublin-fire-brigade-logbook-easter1?e=14465261/10249475).

2   McGarry, *Rebels*, p. 230.

Most of the fires on Sackville Street were caused by the artillery bombardment. However, looters were also reported to have started fires on premises to cover their tracks, or even just for 'fun'. One Volunteer in the Imperial Hotel on the east side of Sackville Street, Kevin McCabe, observed the looting of a boot shop and 'saw a boy and girl in the office lighting a bundle of papers to set fire to the place. I closed the door and threatened to keep them there unless they put out the fire. They beat it out quickly then.'[3] Other would-be arsonists may have been more successful.

As the fires intensified later in the week, Dublin Fire Brigade came under even greater pressure and was assisted by the private fire brigades of the Guinness Brewery and Power's Distillery. On 30 April these combined forces managed to save Jervis Street Hospital from the blaze; afterwards Dublin Fire Brigade was singled out for particular praise by the military authorities and Dublin Corporation, which granted its members a small bonus. The total cost of the damage was estimated at over £2,600,000. Most of the southern end of Sackville Street was destroyed; the buildings that now stand there were, for the most part, newly constructed after the Rising.

Part of a shell taken from the GPO after the Rising. (*Courtesy of Kilmainham Gaol Museum, KMGLM 2015.0309*)

A macabre indication of the human cost of the devastation, as opposed to the financial, was to be seen in the stark red epidemic notices distributed throughout the city after the Rising. They stated that 'persons discovering dead bodies should inform the police or the Chief Medical Officer of Health, Municipal Building, Castle St, immediately'.[4]

---

3   *Ibid.*, p. 177.
4   NLI MS EPH C613: 'Prevention of epidemic'.

38

The Evening Sun, 1 May 1916

Reporting the Rising

The Evening Sun was the evening edition of the New York newspaper the *Sun* (most famous for its 1897 editorial that declared 'Yes Virginia, there is a Santa Claus'). On 1 May 1916, over news of tensions on the USA–Mexican border, the expectation of unrest arising from a massive May Day parade in New York being accompanied by retaliatory strike action in response to lockouts by employers, and reports of German attacks on the Western Front, the newspaper led with the headline '1,200 rebels captured; Dublin loss $10,000,000' and a photograph of Patrick Pearse with the heading 'President of Ireland for five days'.

The Easter Rising was a major story across the Atlantic. News of the Rising appeared on the front page of *The New York Times* every day between 25 April and 8 May, and it received extensive coverage elsewhere. Given the size of Irish communities in cities such as Boston, Chicago and New York (where some of the plans for the Rising had been hatched), it was inevitable that it would be of great interest in the USA. Indeed, considering how and where it had taken place, it was bound to be of considerable import even outside Irish-America. It should be said that the reporting was not automatically positive; the editorial line of *The New York Times* was quite unsympathetic, though the executions also attracted unfavourable comment. Nor was all the coverage accurate. On 25 April *The Evening Sun* reported that the British had recaptured the GPO.

The Evening Sun

HOME EDITION

HOME EDITION

NEW YORK, MONDAY, MAY 1, 1916.

PRICE ONE CENT

1,200 REBELS CAPTURED; DUBLIN LOSS $10,000,000

HOSTS OF LABOR PARADE IN MAY DAY CELEBRATION

Union Leaders Estimate That 200,000 Will Be in Line — Police Prepare to Put Down Violence — 60,000 Needle Workers Out.

THOMPSON WILL RESUME TO-DAY

Says He'll Fix Blame for Subway Cave-In.

BRITISH STEAMSHIP SUNK

PRINCE ALBERT RECOVERS

GIRL KILLED IN JOY RIDE; 4 OTHERS BADLY HURT

Jersey Party's Speeding Car Hits Brick Building.

PRICES ARE STEADY IN THE STOCK MARKET

Moderate Activity Is Shown at the Start.

VILLA BANDS DEFEATED

57 ARRESTED FOR SPEEDING

BORDER PARLEY REACHES CRISIS

Scott to Refuse Obregon's Withdrawal Demand.

NO ULTIMATUM ISSUED

Baker's Reply Secret, but Said to Be Firm.

PRESIDENT OF IRELAND FOR FIVE DAYS

REPORT ON WAY FROM GERARD

Said to Contain Account of Talk With Kaiser.

COUNTESS MARKIEVICZ ARRESTED IN DUBLIN

Woman Leader of Rebels Also Reported Wounded.

FOUR BRITISH GENERALS TAKEN AT KUT-EL-AMARA

Prisoners Also Include 510 Other Officers.

BERLIN DRAFTING REPLY

200 DEAD AND WOUNDED IN SEVEN-DAY REVOLT

Prisoners Taken to England Under Guard — President of "Irish Republic" Wounded Before He Urged Surrender to Troops.

HEAVY GERMAN ASSAULT FAILS

French Repulse Foe North of Dead Man Hill.

SEVERE LOSSES CLAIMED

Rains in Flanders Impede Fighting Armies.

Some of the inaccuracies that marked the early US reports of the Rising may have been due to tight deadlines and a creative willingness to plug gaps. US reporting of the Rising also tended to rely on the reports from London, which in turn were hamstrung by the fact that, as figures like James Stephens were all too aware, newspaper publication in Dublin had ceased during the Rising and would not resume until the beginning of May.

Joe Lee has observed that there are no contemporary Irish newspaper reports of the Easter Rising; all came after the fact, as no dailies were published in Dublin after 27 April. Provincial newspapers, which usually appeared on a Saturday – in this case 29 April – were, like many of their US counterparts, filled with lurid claims of socialist plots and German officers in Dublin. (*The Cork Examiner* and *Roscommon Herald* warmed to these themes and they also appeared in the columns of the *Irish Independent*, though other Irish newspapers took more nuanced views in the immediate aftermath of the Rising.)[1] Even aside from the disruption caused by the Rising, the imposition of martial law would have made it difficult for news to filter out of Dublin. Private accounts, such as that of Wesley Hanna, offer a more revealing picture of events, but these were not meant for the public domain.

For newspapers on both sides of the Atlantic, the disruption caused by the Rising gave some of their coverage a hollow centre. Once the Rising was over, however, newspapers had many opportunities to catch up with events and the spate of special editions and supplements that followed shows that they welcomed the opportunity with open arms.

---

1 J. J. Lee, *Ireland 1912–1985: Politics and Society* (Cambridge, 1989), pp. 28–36.

39

Burial Register for Prospect Cemetery, General Grounds

VICTIMS

According to the Glasnevin Trust, 485 people were killed during, or because of, the Easter Rising; many, if not most, were buried in Glasnevin Cemetery itself. This page from the Glasnevin Burial Register indicates the scale of the task they faced; burials in Glasnevin had virtually come to a halt during the week of the Rising, but the numbers increased enormously in the immediate aftermath.

Of those victims killed between 24 and 29 April, 107 (26 per cent) were members of the British armed forces (including Irish troops). Thirteen (4 per cent) were members of either the DMP or the RIC. Fifty-eight (16 per cent) were members of the insurgent forces and 184 (54 per cent) were civilians. Some of those listed in this page of the general register for what was then Prospect Cemetery come from the inner-city tenements, such as Charlemont Street. Another, William O'Neill, a sixteen-year-old labourer killed by gunfire, was from Church Street. One has to question the rationale of the insurgents in choosing to fight in some of these areas: there was a strategic logic to some of the locations, but had the Volunteers considered the well-being of those living there?

Patrick Pearse brought the Rising to a halt as he felt that their point had been made; that to fight on was to bring further unnecessary suffering on civilians, and certainly, Volunteers like Michael O'Hanrahan, who was part of the garrison in Jacob's biscuit factory, were concerned that their presence might invite devastating attacks on densely populated civilian areas. However, they were the ones who had chosen to establish a presence there.

The decision to fight in Dublin city centre inevitably led to casualties, but if the dead of the Rising were the victims of those fighting, then it must be remembered that the republicans were not the only ones to do that fighting. The vast majority of those involved in the fighting in Dublin were British soldiers. They far outnumbered the insurgents, used far more destructive weapons, were more mobile and were more likely to indiscriminately attack an enemy who was often deemed to be indistinguishable from the general populace. Some of the deaths inflicted by British forces could be put down to nerves and inexperience, some to the orders issued by British commanders to their troops and some can be ascribed to breakdowns in discipline that privately shocked some British officers.

There were also some very calculated killings of civilians. The shooting of the well-known pacifist Francis Sheehy-Skeffington and a number of others in Portobello Barracks is the most famous example of this. The deliberate killing of innocent and unarmed civilians by troops in North King Street, not to mention the subsequent attempts to exonerate the soldiers involved, also shows how the brutality of war came to Dublin and exacted a dreadful toll.

Then there are those whose deaths can be attributed to the circumstances created by the Rising. Take the case of James Gibney (no relation), aged five, of 16 Henrietta Place, who died some days after the Rising, on 2 May 1916 and was buried in Glasnevin (and incorrectly listed as John Gibney). The cause of death was listed as 'probably heart disease & shock. No med. attendant. Inquest unnecessary'. Glasnevin could have made a mistake; equally, his family, who would have known the actual circumstances, may have informed them of the cause as they saw it: 'cannonade'.[1] The family lived near North King Street and Church Street; the area deemed by the British authorities to have been the site of much of the most intense fighting, which almost certainly took a toll on the civilian population. James might not have been killed during the Rising itself, but it is hard not to think that the destruction and disruption that took place in the locality where he and his family lived might have contributed to his death. The death certificate refers to the possibility of an existing heart condition, after all. The cost of fighting extended, as always, far beyond those who actually fought.

---

1 General Register Office: Deaths, April–June 1916.

40

British Public Notice, 11 May 1916

REPRESSION

It must be said again that the Rising was not automatically popular in either Dublin or the rest of Ireland. It came from out of the blue and public opinion most definitely seemed stacked against the insurgents, with hostility cutting across boundaries of politics, religion and class. Outside the capital, even where there was no fighting, similar sentiments could be discerned at a political level and local authorities passed resolutions condemning the Rising.

There were various reasons for this hostility. The families of serving soldiers were particularly outraged at what had happened, and were vocal in their condemnation on the streets. There was also the more straightforward fact that the rebels had brought war to the streets of Dublin, with the disruption that entailed. Many contemporaries were of the view that 'it was as much directed against Home Rule and against Redmond as against England'.[1] At the same time, the fact that an uprising against British rule took place at all seemed to strike a chord with many and the hostility was not universal.

On balance, however, when Easter Week ended it looked as if the Rising had been defeated and could be disregarded as the UK pressed on with the war effort. What really seemed to change public attitudes towards the rebels and their cause was not their actions in themselves: it was how

---

1   O'Farrell, *1916: What the People Saw*, p. 176.

PUBLIC NOTICE

POLITICAL MEETINGS, PARADES, OR PROCESSIONS

I, GENERAL SIR JOHN GRENFELL MAXWELL, K.C.B., K.C.M.G., C.V.O., D.S.O., Commanding-in-Chief His Majesty's Forces in Ireland, hereby Order that no Parade, Procession, or Political Meeting, or organized Football, Athletic, or Hurling Meeting, shall take place anywhere in Ireland without the written authority, previously obtained, of the Local County Inspector of Royal Irish Constabulary, or, in Dublin City, of the Chief Commissioner of the Dublin Metropolitan Police.

J. G. MAXWELL,
*General, Commanding-in-Chief,
The Forces in Ireland.*

HEADQUARTERS, IRISH COMMAND,
11th May, 1916.

(261.) Wt. 557/G. 88. 5,000, 5, '16. FALCONER, DUBLIN.

the British military responded to them. Martial law had been declared in Dublin on Tuesday 25 April and was extended countrywide the next day. This was hardly surprising, given British fears of German involvement in the rebellion. While British officials like Chief Secretary Augustine Birrell counselled against the extension of martial law, military considerations took precedence over political sensitivities.

The public notice pictured here and originally issued by General Sir John Maxwell in his capacity as commander-in-chief (and military governor) on 11 May, banned unauthorised public gatherings that could be turned into political events (at some point the restriction on sports was crossed out). It was issued nearly two weeks after the Rising had come to an end, and the day before the final batch of executions on 12 May. It also applied to the whole of Ireland, not just any district in which fighting had taken place, which suggests that the British response to the Rising was far more sustained, and widespread, than the Rising itself. Maxwell ordered that searches for weapons and suspects be conducted across the entire country, and such indiscriminate (and often heavy-handed) tactics fuelled a sense of resentment towards the British military authorities.

On the same day that this proclamation was issued John Redmond's deputy, John Dillon – who had previously warned Maxwell of the pitfalls of this approach – gave a ferocious speech in the House of Commons in which he accused the government of, amongst other things, 'doing everything conceivable to madden the Irish people'. Dillon had spent Easter Week in Dublin and had a shrewder grasp of its impact than many of his colleagues. 'Would not any sensible statesman think he had enough to do in Dublin and other centres where disturbances broke out, without doing everything possible to raise disturbance and spread disaffection over the whole country?'[2]

The executions that followed the Rising undoubtedly generated

---

2 Townshend, *Easter 1916*, p. 275.

a degree of public sympathy for those killed, but the heavy-handed approach of the British authorities in the weeks and months after the rebellion gave republicans a propaganda victory instead of just a military defeat.

GENERAL MAXWELL AND HIS STAFF, 1916
From left: Capt. the Marquis of Anglesey, Brig.-Gen. Hutchinson, Capt. Bucknill, General Sir J Maxwell, Col. Taylor, Capt. Prince Alexander of Battenberg, Gen. Byrne, and Col. Stanton

General Sir John Maxwell and his staff. Maxwell was the military governor appointed by Herbert Asquith's government to deal with the Rising and its aftermath.
(Courtesy of Kilmainham Gaol Museum, KMGLM 2015.0090)

41

Playing Cards used by Thomas MacDonagh in Captivity

THE EXECUTIONS

Thomas MacDonagh apparently used these playing cards as he awaited execution for his part in the Easter Rising. They are well worn and some missing cards have been replaced. Presumably they provided a distraction in Kilmainham Gaol before his execution by firing squad in the stonebreakers' yard on 3 May.

In many ways the Easter Rising is defined by the executions that came after it: fourteen in Dublin, one in Cork and Roger Casement in London the following August. They are widely seen as a tipping point whereby military defeat began to be transformed into political victory. Up to 1916 Ireland had been governed by a civilian administration based in Dublin Castle, but within days of the Rising General Maxwell was appointed military governor. While he behaved as one might expect in the circumstances, Maxwell took no consideration of Irish political sensitivities, which proved to be disastrous.

In the immediate aftermath, approximately ninety prisoners were sentenced to death in Dublin by short and perfunctory courts martial held in Richmond Barracks under the auspices of the wartime Defence of the Realm Act. Between 3 and 12 May fourteen men were shot by firing squads in Kilmainham Gaol, including the signatories of the Proclamation. Figures such as Tom Clarke and Patrick Pearse seem to have felt that their executions might serve to galvanise Irish opinion in favour of their cause

and, in hindsight, they appear to have had a point. Regardless of what Irish people felt about the Rising, the fact that the British Army had shot Irish prisoners struck a chord with many.

On 11 May the veteran Home Rule MP John Dillon indicted the wartime government in the House of Commons for 'washing out our life's work in a sea of blood … It is not murderers who are being executed; it is insurgents who have fought a clean fight, however misguided, and it would be a damned good thing for you if your soldiers were able to put up as good a fight as did these men in Dublin.'[1]

It quickly became obvious that Maxwell had overstepped the mark and the remaining death sentences were commuted, but the damage was done. Considering what had happened in Dublin – a rebellion that seemed to have had links to Britain's wartime enemy – it is inconceivable that the British authorities would, or could, have taken a lenient approach to those who had planned and participated in the rebellion. However, the political implications of the executions proved to be disastrous.

When combined with the extension of martial law across the entire country in response to a rebellion that was essentially confined to Dublin, along with the mass internment of over 3,500 suspects (far more than had actually taken part in the Rising), it seemed that the British state was adopting an indiscriminate approach to the suppression of the rebellion. The manner of the British response crystallised a range of simmering discontents into more explicit hostility to British rule. The executions were the most notorious example of its heavy-handedness.

This should not detract from the poignancy of the deaths on a human level. MacDonagh, in his cell, composed a statement where he justified his conduct but bemoaned his poor finances and the implications that might have for his family's future: 'the one bitterness that death has for me is the separation it brings from my beloved wife, Muriel, and my beloved

---

1   F. S. L. Lyons, *John Dillon: a Biography* (London, 1968), p. 373.

children, Donagh and Barbara … it breaks my heart to think that I shall never see my children again'.[2] In the end, he never saw his wife again either. Along with Clarke and Pearse, he was executed in Kilmainham on 3 May 1916. Sergeant Major Samuel Lomas, who oversaw their executions, recorded that it 'was sad to think that these three brave men who met their death so bravely should be fighting for a cause which proved to be useless and had been the means of so much bloodshed'.[3]

MacDonagh, like the others executed, was interred in the grounds of Arbour Hill Prison. Built in the 1840s as a military prison, Arbour Hill's gym had been used as a detention centre for many of those captured after the Rising. The fourteen men executed in Dublin were buried in a mass grave with quicklime, originally within the exercise yard of the prison, out of public view. General Maxwell, in response to Margaret Pearse's request for the release of the bodies of her two sons, refused on the grounds that 'Irish sentimentality will turn these graves into martyr's shrines'.[4] Clearly he was not entirely oblivious to the political implications of the executions. Remarkably precise instructions were issued for the interments, and Captain H. V. Stanley of the Royal Army Medical Corps oversaw the burial of MacDonagh, Clarke, Pearse and others. James Connolly's family later singled Stanley out for his courtesy and consideration after he attempted to return Connolly's personal effects to them.

---

2 MacLochlainn (ed.), *Last Words*, p. 61.
3 Mick O'Farrell, *The 1916 Diaries of an Irish Rebel and a British Soldier* (Cork, 2014), p. 183.
4 Brian Barton, *The Secret Court Martial Records of the Easter Rising* (Stroud, 2010), p. 81.

42

Thomas Kent's Rosary Beads
The Rising in Cork

The Catholic Church was profoundly hostile to secret societies, including the Fenians, so it may seem strange that the rebellion orchestrated in 1916 by a new generation of Fenians was carried out, for the most part, by strikingly devout Catholics. However, Irish people who grew up after the Famine were exposed to an aggressively ambitious Catholic Church, and it is to be expected that many of those who fought in the Easter Rising would be committed Christians. Decades of the rosary were recited daily in the GPO and confessions were heard in a number of the garrisons, while the most effective preventative measure against looting seemed to have been the censure of Catholic priests. The rosary beads pictured here belonged to Thomas Kent, and it is understandable that he would have used them to seek solace; he held them just before his execution by firing squad in Victoria Barracks in Cork.

Kent was the only one of the fifteen men shot immediately after the Easter Rising to be executed outside Dublin. The Cork Brigade of the Volunteers, commanded by Tomás MacCurtain, had planned to mobilise at Easter 1916 to rendezvous with the expected landing of arms from the *Aud* in conjunction with their fellow Volunteers in Kerry and Limerick. They did not, however, expect that the landing of these weapons would be the prelude to an immediate uprising. MacCurtain seemed to learn this only in the week before the Rising. He subsequently received a flurry of confusing and contradictory orders from Dublin as to what the Cork Volunteers

Thomas Kent
(*Courtesy of Mercier Archive*)

should do, but given how poorly armed they were, any confrontation with the authorities was a moot point. Over 1,000 Volunteers assembled at various locations in Cork at Easter expecting to collect some of the weapons that were to have been landed from the *Aud*, but they were eventually dismissed by MacCurtain. Some of the Volunteers, however, barricaded themselves into the Cork Volunteer Hall on Sheares Street. Attempts to broker an honourable means of standing down were made by Lord Mayor T. C. Butterfield and the Catholic Archbishop of Cork, Daniel Cohalan. British forces in the city were party to a tentative local agreement based on the temporary handing in of the Volunteers' weapons. MacCurtain was appalled when local newspapers reported, prematurely, that the Cork Volunteers had surrendered their weapons, which was a breach of the agreement. Captain F. W. Dickie, the British officer who oversaw the negotiations, then officially withdrew from the arrangement, possibly after an attack on an RIC barracks in Ballinadee by other members of the Cork Volunteers. Many (though not all) of the weapons were handed in to the authorities as had been agreed, but on 2 May the RIC began looking for members of the Cork Volunteers as part of the general crackdown that followed the Rising. Amongst those wanted by the police were Thomas Kent and his three brothers.

Kent was born near Fermoy in 1865. His family were moderately wealthy farmers; part of the new Catholic middle class that emerged in the

decades after the Great Famine. In his twenties Kent had been a supporter of the Land League and Parnell's Home Rule movement, but had drifted away from active politics until 1914, when he and his brothers joined the newly formed Irish Volunteers. New members of the Volunteers were organised and trained by the Kent brothers (sometimes on the family farm) and Thomas became known to the authorities as a vociferous opponent of recruitment into the British Army during the war.

When the family farm was raided by the RIC on 2 May, a gunfight ensued and Head Constable W. C. Rowe was killed. On the Kents' surrender it seems to have been only the actions of a British officer that prevented RIC men shooting three of the brothers on the spot. David and Richard Kent were wounded (the latter fatally), but Thomas and William Kent were court-martialled. Thomas Kent was convicted and was executed on 9 May in Victoria Barracks. His conviction was dubious; it was not proven that he had killed Rowe. Moreover, the incident took place after the Rising had ended, so were the Kent brothers really rebels, or just resisting arrest?

Thomas Kent was the only member of the Cork Volunteers to be executed, but many more were detained for lengthy periods as official repression continued. Amongst them was his brother David, who was also sentenced to death for his role in the shoot-out, but had his sentence commuted to life imprisonment; he subsequently served as a Sinn Féin MP (and TD) in County Cork.

Detail of the back of the cross on the rosary beads.
(*Courtesy of Cork Public Museum*)

43

Platter used by Sir Roger Casement during his Appeal against his Conviction for Treason, July 1916

The Execution of Sir Roger Casement

When, on 24 April 1916, *The Freeman's Journal* reported that 'a stranger, of unknown nationality' had been arrested in Kerry, it was not in a position to name him. That 'stranger' turned out to be Roger Casement, and he spent no more than thirty-one hours in Kerry before being transferred to London to stand trial. Casement's lengthy and prominent career as a British consular official meant that he was the most well-known figure involved in the Easter Rising; indeed, many of the US newspapers which covered the Rising claimed he was its leader. In reality, by April 1916 Casement was probably more detached from the Rising than any of the others executed in its aftermath.

Casement had spent most of the previous two years in Germany, in a sustained but unsuccessful attempt to persuade the Germans to support a rebellion that he felt was doomed to failure without that support. It was no secret that he was in Germany. He had resigned from the consular service in 1913, and became increasingly active in nationalist activism (witness his role in organising the Howth gun-running). He had also become bitterly critical of British imperial motives and, having travelled to Germany in October 1914, was a wanted man even before the Rising broke out. By April 1916 his health was poor and it was obvious that the Germans

wanted nothing more to do with his proposals. He still favoured the landing of the weapons on the *Aud*, if only because they could be used another day, and he later claimed to have returned to Ireland in an effort to call off the rebellion, but that cut little ice with his British captors. It is hard not to think of his return to Ireland on a U-boat as the act of a man driven to desperation.

Casement was in custody in London by Easter Sunday 1916. He was tried for treason at the Old Bailey in June 1916 according to a statute that dated from 1351, and was convicted on 29 June. The trial lasted for four days, and he was officially stripped of his knighthood the day after his conviction. Given his international reputation as a humanitarian, Casement's trial attracted

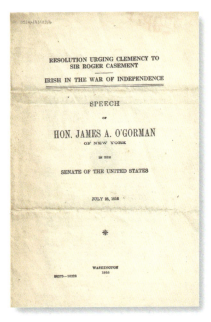

Casement's trial attracted a great deal of publicity. This is the published version of a speech made in the US Senate by James A. O'Gorman (NY), 25 July 1916, arguing for clemency. (*Courtesy of Allen Library, Christian Brothers, Dublin*)

huge attention, but the prospect of an appeal for clemency was deflected by the circulation of what were alleged to be his diaries, detailing a range of homosexual encounters over the course of his career. The authenticity of these diaries has been contested and has never been satisfactorily resolved, but that does not change the fact that they were successfully used against him. By the public standards of Edwardian morality, Casement was deemed to be far worse than merely a traitor.

Casement inevitably appealed his case and that is where the platter pictured here hoves into view. It originally belonged to a pub called the Seven Stars in Carey Street in London, directly behind the Court of Criminal Appeal. Casement's cousins, Gertrude and Elizabeth Bannister, arranged for him to have his meals brought from the pub, and this was the plate that was used. Until the 1960s it was mounted on the wall of the pub with a plaque declaring 'This is the plate from which The Traitor Roger Casement ate his meals on 17 and 18 July 1916'.[1] After the pub changed hands in the mid-1960s it was bought for £1 by John Boland and Proinsias Mac Aonghusa, with the intention of donating it to a Casement museum that was never established; Mac Aonghusa apparently kept it under a bed for the next three decades before donating it to Gaelscoil Mhic Easmainn in Tralee in 1998.

Casement's appeal failed; he was hanged on 3 August 1916 and was buried in Pentonville Prison in London. In 1965 his remains were repatriated to Ireland, to be reinterred in Glasnevin Cemetery.

Roger Casement on the way to his trial. (*Courtesy of Mercier Archive*)

---

1 Lucy McDiarmid, 'Secular Relics: Casement's Boat, Casement's Dish', *Textual Practice*, 16.2 (2002), p. 296.

44

Biscuits given to Kathleen Lynn in Prison

CAPTIVITY

Kathleen Lynn was the daughter of a Church of Ireland cleric in Co. Mayo. She was educated in Britain and Germany and entered the medical profession, becoming a fellow of the Royal College of Surgeons. She was also politically active in campaigns for suffrage and helped to organise soup kitchens for the urban poor during the 1913 Lockout. In 1916 she was the chief medical officer for the ICA and was among the members of the Citizen Army who occupied Dublin City Hall on the first day of the Rising. Given the proximity of City Hall to Dublin Castle, it was captured by troops within a matter of hours, and the surviving members of its garrison, including Lynn, were detained. They were the first to experience what most members of the insurgent garrisons would be faced with within a week: captivity.

The republicans who surrendered were detained in a variety of locations. Those who had been holed up in Moore Street were detained overnight in the garden of the Rotunda Hospital; Richmond Barracks, Arbour Hill Prison and the old Dublin county gaol at Kilmainham were also used as detention centres. It was obvious that the authorities were quite unprepared for the sudden imprisonment of so many (most of the prisoners were eventually detained in England and Wales).

The initial priority of the authorities was to identify the ringleaders, and this was done with the assistance of the police; the welfare of the

prisoners seems to have been overlooked at the start. Even aside from specific accounts of ill-treatment and acts of kindness from their British (and Irish) captors, many prisoners, male and female, reported poor conditions, inadequate sanitary arrangements and bad food.

Lynn and the other members of the garrison in City Hall were detained for about a week in Ship Street Barracks (behind Dublin Castle) and were simply marched through the castle to get to it. At some stage in her captivity, she was given the biscuits pictured here and she left a detailed description of the diet on which she and her fellow prisoners survived:

Dr Kathleen Lynn
(*Courtesy of Kilmainham Gaol Museum, KMGLM 2015.0674*)

> The first day, we had quite a good dinner. After that, the food got slacker and slacker until, in the end, we were getting ship's biscuits and water. That was our diet for several days. I think we were about eight days there. The old military sergeant advised us that, if we moistened a cloth with water and rolled the biscuits in it, it would be easier to eat them, and we did that. He was really a kind old boy. When the military were able to go around a bit, some of them broke into one of the houses nearby; and the sergeant came in one evening with his pockets full of oranges which he gave us. We thought we had never tasted anything so delicious as these oranges.[1]

Lynn claimed to have given some of her ration of biscuits to younger women who were detained and she became quite malnourished during the early stages of her captivity. She and the others were moved to Richmond

---

1   Kathleen Lynn, BMH WS 357, p. 1.

Barracks and Kilmainham Gaol before finally being held in Mountjoy Prison, where 'after a while, we were allowed visitors and parcels, and then we were inundated with all sorts of presents of luxuries. The only thing we longed for was clean bread and butter. We had all sorts of cakes and fruits, etc., but we wanted something plain.'[2]

Lynn was eventually deported to England but returned to Ireland and remained politically active throughout the years that followed. However, her main contribution to Irish life was through her profession, with the establishment of St Ultan's Hospital for infants in 1919; a pioneering venture shaped in part by Lynn's familiarity with the horrific living conditions and appalling child mortality rates that were to be found in Dublin's slums.

British soldiers guarding prisoners, probably at Richmond Barracks.
(*Courtesy of Kilmainham Gaol Museum, KMGLM 2015.0145.01*)

---

2   *Ibid.*, p. 4.

45

Wood Carving made by a Prisoner in Frongoch

FRONGOCH AND THE PRISON EXPERIENCE

Approximately 3,500 Irish men and women were detained for their alleged involvement in the Easter Rising; a far higher number than actually took part in it. Perhaps 1,500 of these were released within a fortnight, as the British authorities realised that they had been somewhat overzealous, but the remainder were detained and sent to a variety of jails across England and Wales. Eventually, the vast majority were transferred to a single location: Frongoch in north Wales, where a former prisoner-of-war camp recently emptied of Germans was used to house the Irish prisoners (it actually consisted of two camps: the 'south' camp was formerly a distillery and was eventually used as a punishment camp).

Initially, Frongoch came as a welcome change to many prisoners who had been detained in the sterner conditions of urban prisons. It was located in a scenic area, the relative isolation of which acted as a security measure in itself, and for the most part the inmates enjoyed a healthy and relaxed environment. While the vast majority of the Irish prisoners had their cases investigated and were subsequently released after interview, by October 1916 Frongoch still had 500 inmates. Given that many of these were committed republicans and members of the IRB and/or the Irish Volunteers, they inevitably began to organise their captivity along military lines and soon came into conflict with the truculent camp commandant, Colonel F. H. Heygate Lambert. He eventually transferred a large number of prisoners to

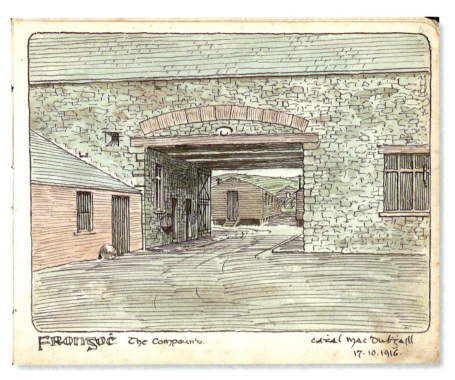

A sketch of Frongoch made by one of the republican prisoners detained there after the Rising: Cathal Mac Dubhgaill (Cecil Grange McDowell), an engineer with Dublin Corporation, who was a member of the 3rd Battalion of the Volunteers under Éamon de Valera. He later arranged the music for Peadar Kearney's *The Soldier's Song*, the Irish version of which, *Amhrán na bhFiann*, was adopted as the Irish national anthem. Mac Dubhgaill was a member of the Church of Ireland but apparently converted to Roman Catholicism during the Rising. In 1921 he married Maeve Kavanagh, whose brother, the *Irish Worker* cartoonist Ernest Kavanagh, was killed outside Liberty Hall during the Rising.
(*Courtesy of Clare Museum*)

the poorer conditions of the south camp for not answering roll calls. The case of the Frongoch prisoners was taken up by Irish Parliamentary Party MPs at Westminster, and inspections of the camp revealed that the conditions in which the prisoners lived had declined markedly since the summer; a fact that was seized on as a propaganda opportunity.

That said, conditions in the camp had been sufficiently relaxed to permit the prisoners to run their own affairs; as the carving depicted here illustrates, they undoubtedly had time on their hands (sports became another favoured pastime). However, Frongoch became an institution in more ways than one; arguably, it was one of the single most important locations of the Irish revolution. By detaining large numbers of republicans and nationalists, and putting many of the most dangerous and committed of them into the same location in Wales, the British inadvertently facilitated the creation of a new republican leadership in the months after the defeat of the Rising. As the Wexford Volunteer leader W. J. Brennan-Whitmore put it, 'the British government had swept up the cream of the Irish Volunteers and dumped them all down in a huge training camp in North Wales'.[1] The executions in May had removed one set of republican leaders; incarceration in Frongoch allowed others, such as Michael Collins and Richard Mulcahy, to emerge and come to prominence. While it suited the camp authorities to have the prisoners running their own affairs, this

Frongoch north camp with Irish prisoners of war.
(*Courtesy of Kilmainham Gaol Museum, 18PC-1D54-04*)

---

1 W. J. Brennan-Whitmore, *With the Irish in Frongoch* (Cork, 2013), p. 47.

also permitted the prisoners to maintain a sense of discipline and purpose. Internment ensured that individuals who may not have been committed republican separatists when they went into jail undoubtedly were when they came out. Furthermore, the bringing together of like-minded individuals who might not otherwise have encountered one another allowed them to forge relationships and networks, and to think ahead to what the next step might be after all the Frongoch prisoners were released – which happened in December 1916. Behind the carvings and sketches made by prisoners to pass the time, the Frongoch experience helped to lay the groundwork for the campaign for independence which intensified after 1918.

46

1916 Memorial Card bought in 17 Moore Street, 1917

Changing Opinions on the Rising

No. 16 Moore Street was owned by a poulterer, Patrick Plunkett, and was the building in which the leaders of the Rising apparently made the final decision to surrender. The building next door, 17 Moore Street, was the premises of R. J. Gore, a chemist who lived in Clontarf. According to a handwritten note on the back, the memorial card pictured here was bought by Gore's assistant 'from a man who came into the shop 17 Moore St Dublin on 19 March 1917 … 11 months before this J. Connolly was carried out of this same house badly wounded afterwards shot with other leaders'.

The card is dedicated, in part, to those same 'leaders'. It began by requesting prayers for the 'repose of the souls of the following Irishmen who were executed by military law, May, 1916'; it then lists the sixteen men who were executed. However, it did not confine itself to them: the card names an additional sixty men 'who were killed whilst fighting for Ireland', and requests prayers for the repose of their souls along with that of Francis Sheehy-Skeffington. The card was produced on behalf the Irish National Aid and Volunteer Dependants' Fund (INAVDF), which was formed by the amalgamation of two charitable organisations established to support prisoners and their families after the Rising.

One of the most striking aspects of the Rising was its immediate afterlife. Despite the hostility it initially attracted in many quarters, by the time the INAVDF was established in August 1916 the authorities were

I gCuimne na hÓglac 'ra ṡṗre

†

Your Prayers

Are Earnestly Requested for the Repose of the Souls of the following Irishmen who were executed by Military Law, May, 1916.

Thomas J. Clarke.	Michael Mallin.
Roger Casement.	Sean M'Dermott.
Eamonn Ceannt.	Thomas M'Donagh.
James Connolly.	John MacBride.
Cornelius Colbert.	Michael O'Hanrahan.
Edward Daly.	Patrick H. Pearse.
J. J. Heuston.	William Pearse.
Thomas Kent.	Joseph Plunkett.

Also for the Repose of the Souls of the following Men who were KILLED WHILST FIGHTING FOR IRELAND During Easter Week, 1916.

John Adams.	Richard Kent
Thomas Allen	Peter Machen
Andrew Byrne	Francis Machen
James Byrne	Peter Manning
Joseph Byrne	Richard Murphy
Frank Burke	D. Murphy
Sean Connolly	Michael Malone
James Corcoran	D. Murray
Harry Coyle	J. McCormack
John Costello	William M'Dowell
John Cromean	The O'Rahilly
John Crinigan	J. O'Reilly
Philip Clarke	Richard O'Reilly
Charles Carrigan	Thomas O'Reilly
Charles Darcy	Richard O'Carroll
Peter Darcy	Patrick O'Flanagan
Brendan Donelan	John O'Grady
Patrick Doyle	J. Owens
John Dwan.	James Quinn
Edward Ennis	Thomas Rafferty
Patrick Farrell	Frederick Ryan
James Fox	George Reynolds
George Geoghegan	Domhnall Sheehan
Sean Howard	Patrick Shortis
John Hurley	John Traynor
John Healy	Edward Walsh
John Kealy	Philip Walsh
Gerald Keogh	Patrick Whelan
John Keily	Thomas Weafer
Con Keating	Peter Wilson

Also for the Repose of the Soul of FRANCIS SHEEHY SKEFFINGTON, who was shot, in Portobello Barracks, April, 1916.

Go nDeinið Dia Trócaire ar a n-anamnaið.

[Issued by the Irish National Aid and Volunteers' Dependants' Fund.] [Gaelic Press, D]

This card was bought by me from a man who came into the shop 17 Moore st dublin on 19 March 1917 where I was at business at the time as chemists assistant to R.G. Goll. 11 months before this J Connolly was carried out of this same house badly wounded afterwards shot with other leaders. on the tuesday after the surrender, con sullivan Royal Irish Rifels. came to this same address just as I got into business to arrest me but it blue over as he was a first cousion to me. I escaped

Michael Keating
Member Irish volenteer
also A.O.H. S.A.A.
North fredrick st

20/3/17

noting that the rebellion was being viewed increasingly sympathetically. Charles Townshend's assessment of why this happened is worth noting: 'The public mood change had two key components. The first ... was condemnation of the military proceedings. The second, equally crucial, was a re-evaluation of the rebels themselves.'[1] 'Sinn Féin' badges became increasingly common; the writings of figures such as Patrick Pearse and James Connolly were republished to meet a burgeoning level of interest; and the Catholicism of the executed men was highlighted by Catholic priests who, despite their Church's traditional hostility towards groups like the IRB, were reported to be fostering sympathy for the executed men as martyrs. This shift in attitudes was a key component of the political changes that happened after the Rising: who could argue with men who had died for Ireland?

Other external factors had a role to play in bringing the separatism of the Rising into the mainstream, but the first steps towards that were those noted by Townshend: revulsion at the heavy-handedness of the British and a more sympathetic 're-evaluation' of the men they had executed. The selling of memorial cards such as this one – and this is only one of many – helped to keep alive the memory of the men who had been executed or who had been killed fighting in the Rising. That memory had a political power. Such sympathy for the dead of the Rising could be, and was, directed into sympathy for separatism.

The man who sold the card in Gore's chemist was, in this case, preaching to the converted: Michael Keating, the chemist's assistant who bought the card, was a member of the Irish Volunteers. He had nearly been arrested in a raid on the premises as he arrived for work on the Tuesday after the Rising. Luckily for Keating, the soldier who had come looking for him was Con Sullivan of the Royal Irish Rifles, his first cousin, and Sullivan seems to have let him off the hook.

---

1   Townshend, *Easter 1916*, p. 308.

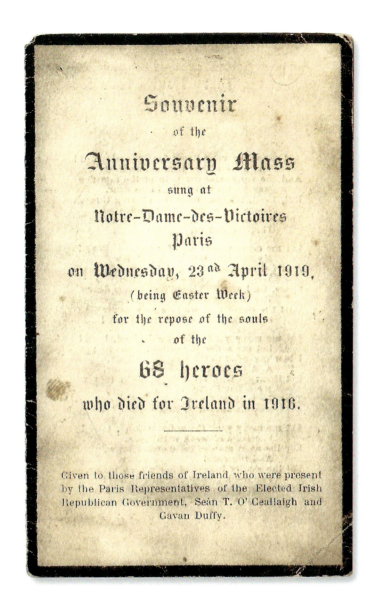

A card for a memorial mass offered on 23 April 1919 in memory of the republican dead of 1916 at Notre-Dame-des-Victoires, Paris. Sinn Féin maintained a presence in Paris in the form of Seán T. O'Kelly and George Gavan Duffy; the card was issued on their behalf as they sought recognition for Irish independence at the post-First World War peace conference.
(*Courtesy of the Allen Library, Christian Brothers, Dublin*)

47

Handcuffs used on Thomas Ashe, 1917

REPUBLICANS AFTER THE RISING

These handcuffs were used on Thomas Ashe during his second, and fatal, sojourn in captivity. Ashe was sentenced to death after the Rising for his role in events in Co. Meath and north Co. Dublin, most especially the attack on the RIC barracks at Ashbourne. Like most of the death sentences, his was commuted to life imprisonment. He was released as part of the general amnesty for republican prisoners in June 1917 and subsequently became president of the supreme council of the IRB. He was enormously popular amongst republicans and campaigned for Éamon de Valera (with whom he had been imprisoned in Lewes Prison after the Rising) in the East Clare by-election caused by the death of the sitting Irish Parliamentary Party MP Willie Redmond. Willie, John Redmond's brother, had joined the British Army on the outbreak of the First World War and was killed at the Battle of Messines in June 1917. Ashe was also involved in re-organising the Irish Volunteers after 1916, but he was arrested under the wartime Defence of the Realm Act after giving a 'seditious' speech in Longford in August and received a two-year prison sentence for his trouble. He was imprisoned in Mountjoy, and was one of forty prisoners detained under the same Act who began a hunger strike on 20 September demanding to be recognised as prisoners of war. The handcuffs pictured here were used on him at this time.

The hunger strikers were forcefed: they were strapped into a chair and a tube was inserted through the nose or mouth into the stomach. Ashe

was forcefed for the first time on 23 September. On 25 September an inexperienced doctor, who apparently was very rough, inserted the feeding tube. Instead of going into his stomach, it entered his lung and due to the force with which it was administered it burst through his lung (bruises were found around Ashe's mouth, which indicates that force was used). He died that night in the Mater Hospital, having been ministered to by the Capuchin Friars who gave the last rites to the 1916 dead, and cared for by Kathleen Lynn.

The prisoners' demands were met within a matter of days (though the forcefeeding continued in the interim). Ashe's funeral on 30 September was a massive event; bigger, according to the *Irish Independent*, than even that of Charles Stewart Parnell in 1891. Ashe lay in state in City Hall before the cortège travelled to Glasnevin Cemetery: huge numbers lined the route.

At the graveside a volley of shots was fired and Michael Collins gave an exceptionally short oration: 'Nothing additional remains to be said. That volley which we have just heard is the only speech it is proper to make over the grave of a dead Fenian.'[1] It may have been shorter than the oration that Patrick Pearse made at O'Donovan Rossa's funeral

Thomas Ashe
(*private collection*)

---

1 Hopkinson, 'Michael Collins', in *Dictionary of Irish Biography*.

in 1915, but the essential purpose was the same. Just as Pearse used his speech to bring militant republicanism back into the limelight, so too did Collins. Ashe was a veteran of 1916; his funeral thus became a link with the independence struggle that was to follow.

Funeral procession for Thomas Ashe, Ormond Quay.
(*Courtesy of Kilmainham Gaol Museum, 18PC-1A45-04*)

48

Letter from Michael Collins to Patrick Fogarty giving Notice of Compensation for Imprisonment, 1917

FROM EASTER RISING TO WAR OF INDEPENDENCE

This letter, dated 21 June 1917, accompanied a cheque from the INAVDF for the not inconsiderable sum of £20 sent to Patrick Fogarty, a Dublin member of the Irish Volunteers, who had been imprisoned after the Rising. The money, it stated, would allow Fogarty 'to take a short holiday after your very trying time'. It seems, however, that the prison regime was not onerous, and that one of the enemies faced by Fogarty and his fellow prisoners was boredom ('we are allowed to talk and it helps to shorten the day'); in January 1917 he asked his mother for Irish grammar books, presumably to help him occupy his time.[1]

The INAVDF looked after its charges; writing to his mother from Lewes Prison in Sussex in December 1916, Fogarty had observed that 'we know that all the men's wives, and those that they supported are very well look [*sic*] after'.[2] The letter that the INAVDF sent to Fogarty ended by stating that 'The Executive hope in three or four weeks time to have an opportunity of discussing with you the arrangements for your future.' The

---

1   Allen Library, Patrick Fogarty papers: IE/AL/PF/4 (22 January 1917).
2   *Ibid.*, IE/AL/PF/3 (21 December 1916).

Comhlucht Congantá na nGaodhal agus Spleadhach Óglach na hÉireann
Longphort: 10 SRÁID AN CISTE, ÁT CLIAT.

Irish National Aid AND Volunteer Dependents' Fund
Offices: 10 EXCHEQUER ST., DUBLIN.

21st June, 1917.

A chara,

I am directed by the Executive to beg your acceptance of the enclosed cheque for £20-0-0 as a preliminary grant which they trust will enable you to take a short holiday after your very trying time. The members of the Executive, one and all, ask me to convey their earnest wishes that you will soon completely recover from the effects of the suffering you have undergone for Ireland. The Executive hope in three or four weeks time to have an opportunity of discussing with you the arrangements for your future.

Do chara,

Mícheál O Coileaín

Mr. Patrick Fogarty.

Patrick Fogarty
(Courtesy of the Allen Library, Christian Brothers, Dublin)

INAVDF subsequently invited him to a reception for released prisoners of war in Dublin's Mansion House three weeks later, on 14 July 1917. Considering the signature at the bottom of the letter, the assurance that Fogarty's future was up for discussion seems pregnant in hindsight; it was signed by the secretary of the INAVDF, Míceál Ó Coilean – Michael Collins – whose remarkable rise to prominence as a key figure in the independence movement after 1916 had begun during his own incarceration in Frongoch. It is quite possible that the two men were acquainted; Collins and Fogarty had a mutual friend in Harry Boland, with whom Fogarty had been imprisoned.

By the summer of 1917 all of those imprisoned or interned after the Rising had been released, but in the camps a new generation of more militant leaders had emerged. The energetic Collins was the most prominent of these and his role in both the INAVDF and the IRB gave him the perfect opportunity to influence the growth of a new republican movement. While imprisoned 1916 veterans like Collins were prepared to support the revamped Sinn Féin, as they were released they also threw their weight behind the reorganisation of the Irish Volunteers and their transformation into the Irish Republican Army (IRA).

The IRA was a young man's organisation, with many of its members drawn from the Catholic lower middle classes (Fogarty himself was a devout Catholic, as were many of his peers). The Volunteers were reorganised in late 1917 and benefited hugely from the wave of popular unease prompted by the prospect of conscription being imposed on Ireland in early 1918. The IRA's stock in trade was ambush and assassination: a far cry from the set-piece fighting of the Easter Rising, and a pragmatic solution to the fact that their enemy was far more formidable than they were. Yet the Easter

Rising was the catalyst for the eventual creation of this new movement and, regardless of the differences between them, there was a good deal of continuity in terms of the people who fought in 1916 and in the later conflict. Fogarty was one of them: he died of pneumonia in April 1920, having contracted it while on active service as a member of the IRA.

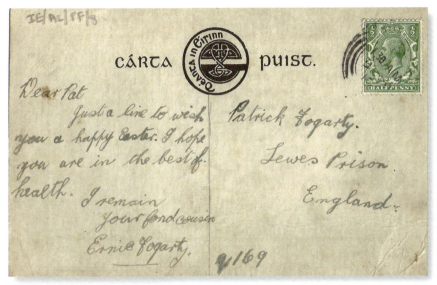

A postcard sent to Patrick Fogarty, by his cousin, while he was imprisoned in Lewes Prison in Sussex after the Rising. (*Courtesy of the Allen Library, Christian Brothers, Dublin*)

49

'Up De Valera', 'Up Griffith': Sinn Féin Badges from the 1918 General Election

THE VICTORY OF SINN FÉIN, 1918

These simple paper election badges date from the first post-war election in 1918. The candidates in question were the Dublin journalist Arthur Griffith and the New York-born maths teacher Éamon de Valera, the commandant of the Volunteer garrison at Boland's Bakery in 1916 who had been sentenced to death after the Rising and whose sentence had been commuted. Given that de Valera was born in New York, it is often assumed that his American citizenship saved him (though that had not saved Tom Clarke). De Valera's private view on the matter was that he had simply been lucky. Having been overlooked for execution, he became a figurehead after the Rising as the most senior of the surviving combatants.

The election was for Westminster and the party they were members of was Sinn Féin, founded in 1905 by Griffith. The original version of Sinn Féin espoused a form of Irish independence under a 'dual monarchy' shared with Britain, based on the Austro-Hungarian model and placing great emphasis on economic self-sufficiency; the name meant 'our selves'. It had never commanded much electoral support, but this does not reflect the enormous influence that the energetic and pugnacious Griffith had on younger nationalists. Over time, 'Sinn Féin' came to be adopted as a catch-all term to describe more radical nationalists. It was probably inevitable

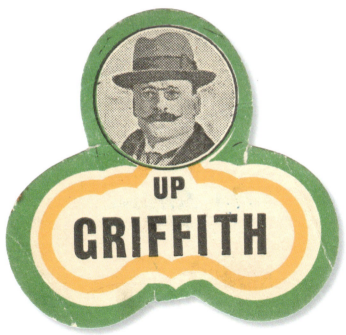

that when the Easter Rising broke out, it was erroneously declared by both onlookers (such as Wesley Hanna) and the authorities to be the 'Sinn Féin Rebellion'. This meant that as Irish opinion began to shift towards the separatism of the Rising, the separatists who had survived had a banner under which to regroup.

The rise of Sinn Féin in the years after 1916 was also related to the collapse of the Home Rule cause. Many contemporaries felt that the Rising was a blow struck at Redmondite nationalism, as much as at the British. In 1917 an 'Irish Convention' was hurriedly convened in Trinity College, Dublin to secure some agreement between nationalists and unionists to allow the implementation of Home Rule. Its failure further discredited a party that was already tainted by Redmond's vociferous support for an increasingly costly war. There is a case to be made that elements of the Irish nationalist electorate may have been open to the prospect of new political representatives, and republicans certainly spotted a gap in the market. In October 1917 Sinn Féin was officially reorganised as a political party committed to the pursuit of an independent Irish Republic (subject to the self-determination of the Irish people), and de Valera was installed as its president. Its specific aims were somewhat vague, but there could be no question about what it was actually against. A vote for Sinn Féin was a vote for something more than Home Rule.

Sinn Féin received its greatest boost in the spring of 1918, when German breakthroughs on the Western Front meant that there was a very real prospect of conscription being extended to Ireland. This prospect caused outrage amongst virtually all shades of nationalist opinion and was opposed by the Catholic Church, Home Rulers, the labour movement (who organised a general strike in protest against it) and, above all, Sinn Féin. It was Sinn Féin who reaped the benefits, and when a general election was held in December 1918 they won seventy-three seats in Westminster, leaving the Home Rulers with six. The fact that the electorate had been extended thanks to franchise reform hardly helped the Home Ruler's case:

first-time voters (including women over thirty) seemed to cast their lot in with the new party.

Sinn Féin candidates had said that, if elected, they would not actually go to Westminster and would instead set up an assembly of their own in Dublin. This was a moot point for de Valera and Griffith, as both of them were in prison at the time of the election on trumped-up allegations that they – and seventy-one others who were also imprisoned – had been conspiring with the Germans. De Valera was returned for the East Clare constituency, unopposed, from the confines of Lincoln Jail; the paper badge reminded the people of East Clare what the man they didn't have to vote for actually looked like. Griffith, who was detained in Gloucester Prison, was returned unopposed for Cavan East, but was also elected as the MP for Tyrone North-West, defeating a unionist candidate by a margin of ten to seven; presumably, the badges did not go to waste there. Instead of going to Westminster – or not going, as the case may be – on 21 January 1919 those newly elected Sinn Féin MPs who were still at liberty assembled at Dublin's Mansion House under the banner of Dáil Éireann and declared Ireland independent.

Sinn Féin argued that as the Great War had supposedly been fought for the rights of small nations, and as they now commanded mass support, they would press for recognition of an Irish Republic at the post-war peace conference. Yet this propaganda drive was accompanied by a new, or renewed, conflict. On the same day as the Dáil met, in an unconnected development, members of the IRA attacked a police patrol in Co. Tipperary. The republican campaign for Irish independence had entered a new phase.

50

Sigerson Monument, Glasnevin Cemetery

The Contested Legacies of the Rising

Dora Sigerson was an Irish writer and artist who was an active figure in the literary revival of the early twentieth century. She married the journalist Clement Shorter in 1895 (sometimes publishing as Dora Sigerson Shorter afterwards), and lived in England for the remainder of her life. She was, however, an Irish nationalist and was deeply affected by the Easter Rising; a posthumous collection of her poems, *16 Dead Men*, consisted of poems dedicated to the sixteen men executed after the Rising. She herself died in 1918 and was buried in Glasnevin Cemetery. Before she died, however, she designed a memorial to the republicans who had been killed during the Rising and left a substantial bequest in her will to have it erected.

The Sigerson Monument stands near the gate of Glasnevin Cemetery (it was relocated there in 2007). It depicts two figures: a female personification of Ireland (modelled on Michelangelo's *Pietà* in St Peter's Basilica in Rome), and the prone figure of a man, the face of which was modelled on Patrick Pearse. One of her poems, 'The Sacred Fire', was inscribed on the rear of the monument:

> They lit a fire within their land that long was ashes cold,
> With splendid dreams they made it glow, threw in their hearts of gold.
> They saw thy slowly paling cheek and knew thy failing breath,
> They bade thee live once more, Kathleen, who wert so nigh to death.

And who dare quench the sacred fire, and who dare give them blame,
Since he who draws too near the glow shall break into a flame?
They lit a beacon in their land, built of the souls of men,
To make thee warm once more, Kathleen, to bid thee live again.

It is often assumed that the commemoration and remembrance of the Easter Rising took a simplistic, eulogistic form in the years after the event. Undoubtedly, on occasion, this was the case. Yet criticisms of the Rising, including by many of those who actually took part in it, can be traced back to the Rising itself, and the meaning of Easter 1916 has been equally contested since it took place. The history of the Sigerson Monument testifies to that.

In the 1920s Dora Sigerson Shorter's husband, Clement, offered to provide £1,000 from her will to permit the erection of the monument. The proposal was put to the executive council of the Irish Free State, which was the government of the independent Irish state that had been established by the Anglo-Irish Treaty of December 1921 and which had emerged victorious but bruised from the Civil War fought over the terms of that treaty in 1922–23. For those defeated republicans who had lost the Civil War, the very existence of the Free State was living proof that the objective of full independence, as demanded and fought for by those who took part in the Rising, had not yet been attained. At the same time, the leader of the government that such republicans viewed as traitors was a veteran of the Rising himself: the former Sinn Féin alderman and abstentionist MP William T. Cosgrave, who had fought alongside Éamonn Ceannt at the South Dublin Union. Cosgrave's government, prepared as it was to rule within the prescriptions set out in the Anglo-Irish Treaty, was wary of accepting Shorter's offer (lest it 'look as if we wanted to have one last slap at the British'), but agreed to the proposal in December 1925.[1]

---

1 David Fitzpatrick, 'Commemoration in the Irish Free State: a Chronicle of

The suggested location of the monument in Glasnevin then proved contentious, as one of the original sites would have obscured Arthur Griffith's grave. Griffith had helped to negotiate the Treaty and briefly headed the new independent government before his premature death, being succeeded by Cosgrave. The fact that Cosgrave and his government were unwilling to countenance any possible slight to Griffith's grave indicates that they did not see their genealogy as consisting of 1916 to the exclusion of all else.

Many republicans took a very different view. The Easter Rising was to be elevated and eulogised not only because it was part of the recent past, but also because it might yet form the basis of a possible future. It symbolised unfinished business, the legacy of which had been sullied in the eyes of many republicans by the willingness of men like Cosgrave, Griffith and Michael Collins to accept something that fell far short of what Patrick Pearse had proclaimed outside the GPO in April 1916.

Cosgrave's government did agree to the suggestion that a parchment scroll with the names of the republican dead of 1916 be encased within the monument, but in May 1927 they decided against any official public unveiling, lest it be a magnet for controversy. When they had held their first official military ceremony to commemorate the Rising in 1924, the only relative to accept an invitation was the widow of the ICA leader Michael Mallin. In 1925 the government simply did not invite any anti-Treaty republicans to that year's commemoration in Arbour Hill military cemetery, where the executed leaders were buried; instead, a rival event took place at Glasnevin Cemetery, and the twain did not meet. Any commemoration of the Easter Rising raises the prospect of various individuals and organisations attempting to claim the mantle of its legacy for themselves. As the story of the Sigerson Monument and other attempts to commemorate the Rising suggest, perhaps it has and will ever be so.

Embarrassment', in Ian McBride (ed.), *History and Memory in Modern Ireland* (Cambridge, 2001), p. 196.

Later generations of republicans would continue to claim inspiration from the events of 1916. This is a copy of the 1916 Proclamation issued with an accompanying manifesto signed by the IRA Army Council *c.* 1939. It was presumably published as the IRA embarked on a renewed bombing campaign in Britain at the outset of the Second World War: the attempt to emphasise the continuity with 1916 should be obvious and was surely strengthened by the fact that the text on the right was signed by George Plunkett, a 1916 veteran and the younger brother of Joseph Plunkett, who was one of the signatories of the original proclamation.

(*Courtesy of Kilmainham Gaol Museum, KMGLM 2015.0319*)

Picture Credits for Main Images

2. Abbey Theatre programme for a play by Thomas MacDonagh: *Courtesy of the Abbey Theatre*

48. Letter from Michael Collins to Patrick Fogarty giving notice of compensation for imprisonment, 1917: *Courtesy of the Allen Library, Christian Brothers, Dublin*

8. Diarmuid Lynch's Irish Volunteer uniform, **18**. Proclamation of the Irish Republic, **38**. *The Evening Sun*, 1 May 1916, **42**. Thomas Kent's rosary beads: *Courtesy of Cork Public Museum*

43. Platter used by Sir Roger Casement during his appeal against his conviction for treason, July 1916: *Courtesy of Gaelscoil Mhic Easmainn, Tralee; photo by Brian Caball*

23. Memorial cup awarded for the defence of Trinity College, Dublin, **26**. Certificate of service for the 16th (Irish) Division, 27 April 1916, **39**. Burial Register for Prospect Cemetery, General Grounds, **50**. Sigerson Monument, Glasnevin Cemetery: *Courtesy of the Glasnevin Trust*

5. Bill from St Enda's to Éamonn Ceannt: *Courtesy of the Jackie Clarke Collection*

16. Mobilisation order for 'B' Company, 1st Battalion, Dublin Brigade, Irish Volunteers, 24 April 1916 (KMGLM 2015.0306), **27**. Compensation claim for damage to 73 and 73a Lower Mount Street (KMGLM 2015.0316.01), **34**. Handkerchief embroidered in Marrowbone Lane, 30 April 1916 (KMGLM 2015.0310), **40**. British public notice, 11 May 1916 (KMGLM 2015.0312), **46**. 1916 memorial card bought in 17 Moore Street, 1917 (KMGLM 2015.0317), **49**. 'Up De Valera' and 'Up Griffith' Sinn Féin badges from the 1918 general election (KMGLM 2011.0481 and 2011.0482): *Courtesy of Kilmainham Gaol Museum*

37. Dublin Fire Brigade helmet: *Courtesy of Las Fallon, private collection*

36. A book damaged by gunfire from Marsh's Library: *Courtesy of the Governors and Guardians of Marsh's Library; photo by Gillian Buckley*

6. Solemn League and Covenant: *Courtesy of Mercier Archive*

24. Wesley Hanna's account of the Rising: *Courtesy of Michael Hanna, private collection; image by Letters of 1916*

17. Poster for the Coliseum Theatre, **25**. Watercolour sketch of a barricade at the Shelbourne Hotel: *Courtesy of the National Library of Ireland*

1. Tom Clarke's certificate of US naturalisation, **7**. Irish Citizen Army flag, **9**. Cumann na mBan brooch, **10**. Baton used in the Howth gun-running, **11**. Irish National Volunteer's uniform, **13**. Uniform for Roger Casement's 'Irish Brigade', **14**. Mosin-Nagant rifle from the *Aud*, 24 April 1916, **19**. Irish Republic flag, **20**. *Irish War News*, **21**. Homemade bomb, **22**. Cricket bat that died for Ireland, **28**. Fianna hat belonging to Seán Healy, **29**: Royal Irish Constabulary Carbine from the Battle of Ashbourne, **30**. Globe belonging to Liam Mellows, **31**. James Connolly's blood-stained shirt, **32**. Artefacts from the *Helga*, **33**. Rubble and cartridges from the GPO, **35**. A fragment of a wall from 16 Moore Street inscribed by Thomas Clarke, **41**. Playing cards used by Thomas MacDonagh in captivity, **47**. Handcuffs used on Thomas Ashe, 1917: *Courtesy of the National Museum of Ireland*

3. Seán MacDiarmada's hurley, **44**. Biscuits given to Kathleen Lynn in prison; **45**. Wood carving made by a prisoner in Frongoch: *Courtesy of the National Museum of Ireland (Brother Allen Collection)*

4. *An Scoláire*: St Enda's student magazine, **12**. Manuscript of Patrick Pearse's oration at the funeral of Jeremiah O'Donovan Rossa, **15**. Teacups used by the Pearse brothers: *Courtesy of the Pearse Museum*

Select Bibliography

Books and articles

1916 Rebellion Handbook (Belfast, 1998)

Barton, Brian, *The Secret Court Martial Records of the Easter Rising* (Stroud, 2010)

Bateson, Ray, *They Died by Pearse's Side* (Dublin, 2010)

Brennan-Whitmore, W. J., *With the Irish in Frongoch* (Cork, 2013)

Campbell, Fergus, 'The Easter Rising in Galway', *History Ireland*, 14.2 (2006), 22–5

Casement, Roger, 'A Last Page of my Diary', ed. Angus Mitchell, *Field Day Review*, 8 (2012), 47–83

Clare, Anne, *Unlikely Rebels: The Gifford Girls and the Fight for Irish Freedom* (Cork, 2011)

Collins, Michael, *The Path to Freedom* (Cork, 2012)

Crowley, Brian, *Patrick Pearse: a Life in Pictures* (Cork, 2014)

Curry, James, *Artist of the Revolution: the Cartoons of Ernest Kavanagh (1884–1916)* (Cork, 2012)

Dictionary of Irish Biography (9 vols, Cambridge, 2009)

Duffy, Joe, 'Children of the Revolution', *History Ireland*, 21.3 (2013), 34–5

Dwyer, T. Ryle, *Michael Collins: the Man Who Won the War* (Cork, 2009)

Fallon, Las, *Dublin Fire Brigade and the Irish Revolution* (Dublin, 2012)

Ferguson, Stephen, *GPO Staff in 1916: Business as Usual* (Cork, 2012)

— *The GPO: 200 Years of History* (Cork, 2014)

Ferriter, Diarmaid, *A Nation and not a Rabble: the Irish Revolution, 1913–1923* (London, 2015)

Fitzpatrick, David, 'Commemoration in the Irish Free State: a Chronicle of Embarrassment', in Ian McBride (ed.), *History and Memory in Modern Ireland* (Cambridge, 2001), 184–203.

Fitzpatrick, Georgina, *Trinity College Dublin and Irish Society, 1914–1922: a Selection of Documents* (Dublin, 1992)

Foster, R. F., *Vivid Faces: the Revolutionary Generation in Ireland, 1891–1923* (London, 2014)

Gibney, John, *16 Lives: Seán Heuston* (Dublin, 2013)

Gillis, Liz, *Revolution in Dublin: A Photographic History, 1913–23* (Cork, 2013)

— *Women of the Irish Revolution* (Cork, 2014)

Good, Joe, *Inside the GPO: a First-hand Account* (Dublin, 2015)

Henry, William, *Supreme Sacrifice: The Story of Éamonn Ceannt* (Cork, 2005)

Jeffrey, Keith, *Ireland and the First World War* (Cambridge, 2000)

Joye, Lar, 'The Irish Volunteer Uniform', *History Ireland*, 21.6 (2013), 37

— 'TSS *Helga*', *History Ireland*, 18.2 (2010), 39

Kenna, Shane, *16 Lives: Thomas MacDonagh* (Dublin, 2014)

Kennerk, Barry, *Moore Street: the Story of Dublin's Market District* (Cork, 2013)

Kildea, Jeff, *Anzacs and Ireland* (Cork, 2007)

Lee, J. J., *Ireland 1912–1985: Politics and Society* (Cambridge, 1989)

Luce, J. V., *Trinity College Dublin: the First 400 Years* (Dublin, 1992)

Lyons, F. S. L., *John Dillon: a Biography* (London, 1968)

MacLochlainn, Piaras F., *Last Words: Letters and Statements of the Leaders Executed after the Rising at Easter 1916* (Dublin, 1990)

Matthews, Ann, 'Vanguard of the Revolution? The Irish Citizen Army, 1916' in Ruán O'Donnell (ed.), *The Impact of the 1916 Rising: Among the Nations* (Dublin, 2008), 24–36

— *The Kimmage Garrison: Making Billy-can Bombs at Larkfield* (Dublin, 2010)

— *Renegades: Irish Republican Women, 1900–1922* (Cork, 2010)

— *Dissidents: Irish Republican Women, 1923–1941* (Cork, 2012)

— *The Irish Citizen Army* (Cork, 2014)

McCarthy, Muriel, *Marsh's Library: All Graduates and Gentlemen* (Dublin, 2003)

McDiarmid, Lucy, 'Secular Relics: Casement's Boat, Casement's Dish', *Textual Practice*, 16.2 (2002), 277–302

McElligott, Jason, 'In the Line of Fire', *History Ireland*, 20.3 (2012), 44–5

McGarry, Fearghal, *The Rising: Easter 1916* (Oxford, 2010)

— *Rebels: Voices from the Easter Rising* (London, 2011)

— 'Violence and the Easter Rising', in David Fitzpatrick (ed.), *Terror in Ireland, 1916–23* (Dublin, 2012), 39–57

— '1916 and Irish Republicanism: Between Myth and History', in John Horne and Edward Madigan (eds), *Towards Commemoration: Ireland in War and Revolution, 1912–1923* (Dublin, 2013), 46–53

McGough, Eileen, *Diarmuid Lynch: A Forgotten Irish Patriot* (Cork, 2013)

McMahon, Sean, *Rebel Ireland: Easter Rising to Civil War* (Cork, 2001)

McNamara, Conor, '"The most shoneen town in Ireland": Galway in 1916', *History Ireland*, 19.1 (2011), 34–7

Mitchell, Angus, *Roger Casement* (Dublin, 2013)

O'Brien, Paul, *Blood on the Streets: 1916 and the Battle for Mount Street Bridge* (Cork, 2008)

— *Uncommon Valour: 1916 and the Battle for the South Dublin Union* (Cork, 2010)

O'Callaghan, John, *16 Lives: Con Colbert* (Dublin, 2015)

Ó Comhraí, Cormac, *Revolution in Connacht: A Photographic History, 1913–23* (Cork, 2013)

— *Ireland and the First World War: a Photographic History* (Cork, 2014)

O'Farrell, Elizabeth, 'Miss Elizabeth O'Farrell's Story of the Surrender', *Catholic Bulletin*, vii (1917), 266–70

O'Farrell, Mick, *A Walk through Rebel Dublin* (Cork, 1994)

— *50 Things You Didn't Know about 1916* (Cork, 2009)

— *1916: What the People Saw* (Cork, 2013)

— *The 1916 Diaries of an Irish Rebel and a British Soldier* (Cork, 2014)

Ó Ruairc, Pádraig Óg, *Revolution: a Photographic History of Revolutionary Ireland, 1913–23* (Cork, 2011)

Pearse, Patrick, *The Coming Revolution* (Cork, 2011)

Rains, Stephanie, *Commodity Culture and Social Class in Dublin, 1850–1916* (Dublin, 2010)

Royal Commission on the Rebellion in Ireland: Report of Commission (London, 1916)

Ryan, Anne-Marie, *16 Dead Men: The Easter Rising Executions* (Cork, 2014)

Ryan, Philip B., *The Lost Theatres of Dublin* (Westbury, 1998)

Sisson, Elaine, *Pearse's Patriots: St Enda's and the Cult of Boyhood* (Cork, 2004)

Stephens, James, *The Insurrection in Dublin* (Gerrards Cross, 1992)

Townshend, Charles, *Easter 1916: the Irish Rebellion* (London, 2005)

White, Gerry and Brendan O'Shea, *Baptised in Blood: The Formation of the Cork Brigade of Irish Volunteers, 1913–16* (Cork, 2005)

— 'Easter 1916 in Cork: Order, Counter-order and Disorder', in Gabriel Doherty and Dermot Keogh (eds), *1916: The Long Revolution* (Cork, 2007), 169–96

Wills, Clair, *Dublin 1916: the Siege of the GPO* (London, 2009)

Yeates, Padraig, *A City in Wartime: Dublin 1914–1918* (Dublin, 2011)

Databases and online resources

Bureau of Military History: www.bureauofmilitaryhistory.ie

Century Ireland: www.rte.ie/centuryireland/

Glasnevin Trust 1916 Necrology: www.glasnevintrust.ie/visit-glasnevin/news/1916-list/

International Encyclopedia of the First World War: www.1914-1918-online.net

Letters of 1916: http://dh.tcd.ie/letters1916/

The Cricket Bat that Died for Ireland: http://thecricketbatthatdiedforireland.com

Index

16th (Irish) Division 119–122

A

Abbey Theatre 16, 18, 19, 38, 80
An Scoláire 24–26
Asgard 48, 50
Ashbourne 130–133, 200
Ashe, Thomas 130, 132, 133, 200–203
Asquith, Herbert H. 9, 33, 174
Aud 64–68, 73, 76, 81, 97, 136, 149, 179, 180, 185

B

Bailey, Daniel 62
Ballykissane Pier 68, 81
Banna Strand 63
Birrell, Augustine 114, 116, 173
Boland's Bakery 95, 123, 125, 143, 208
Brady, Christopher 83, 85
Brennan-Whitmore, W. J. 194
Brugha, Cathal 150

C

Carson, Edward 34, 59, 104
Casement, Roger 48, 60–64, 81, 95, 112, 175, 183–186
Ceannt, Éamonn 28–30, 85, 150, 214
Childers, Erskine 48, 50
City Hall 38, 58, 95, 187, 189, 202
Clan na Gael 14, 58
Clanwilliam House 125
Clarke, Kathleen 14, 157
Clarke, Thomas J. 11–15, 22, 23, 54, 58, 59, 70, 73, 76, 83, 86, 90, 140, 154–157, 175, 178, 208
Colbert, Con 26, 127, 129, 152, 153
Coliseum Theatre 78, 80, 82
College Green 106, 108, 160
Collins, Michael 156, 194, 202–204, 206, 215
Connolly, James 15, 36, 38, 39, 83, 85, 86, 88, 90, 93, 138–141, 156, 157, 178, 196, 198
Connolly, Seán 38
Cork city 7, 16, 38, 40, 42, 77, 122, 175, 179, 180, 182
Cosgrave, Marcella 47
Cosgrave, William T. 214, 215
Craig, James 34
Cumann na mBan 44–47, 51, 87, 152, 157
Cusack, Michael 20

D

Dáil Éireann 211
Daly, Edward 73
Davin, Maurice 20
de Valera, Éamon 46, 123, 125, 143, 193, 200, 208–211
Devoy, John 14, 58, 60, 62
Dillon, John 173, 177
Donegan, Seamus 156
Dublin Castle 38, 95, 117, 140, 175, 187, 189
Dublin Fire Brigade 161–164
Dublin Metropolitan Police (DMP) 38, 39, 51, 90, 101, 106, 158, 168

E

Enniscorthy 7, 76
Evening Sun, The 165–167

F

Fianna Éireann, Na 26, 48, 50, 51, 127–129, 134, 152
Fitzgerald, Theo 88
Flood, Robert 153
Fogarty, Patrick 204–207
Four Courts 95, 96, 132
Freeman's Journal, The 81, 183
Frongoch 133, 137, 191–195, 206

G

Gaelic Athletic Association (GAA) 20–23, 30, 82, 130, 134
Gaelic League 17, 28, 40, 42, 69, 71, 130, 152
Galway 7, 20, 28, 67, 77, 132, 134–137

General Post Office
(GPO) 7, 40, 80, 82,
85, 86, 88–92, 93,
95, 100, 101, 108,
130, 138, 140, 144,
146–149, 154, 157,
163–165, 179, 215
Gibney, James 170
Glasnevin (Prospect)
Cemetery 56, 58, 129,
168–170, 186, 202,
212, 215
Golden, David 62
Good, Joe 98, 144, 146,
148, 156
Gore, R. J. 196
Griffith, Arthur 106,
208–211, 215

H

Hanna, Wesley 110–113,
167, 210
Healy, Michael 114
Healy, Seán 127–129
Helga 142–145
Henry Street 78, 103, 149,
154
Heuston Seán 51
Heuston, Seán 48, 50,
119, 127
Heygate Lambert, F. H.
191
Hobson, Bulmer 26, 42,
48, 127, 140, 141
Holland, Bob 152, 153
Holohan, Garry 129
Holohan, Paddy 129
Home Rule 8, 9, 11, 17,
22, 31, 33, 34, 36, 40,
43, 44, 52, 70, 95, 140,
171, 177, 182, 210
Howth 48, 50, 51, 60, 127,
132, 183
Hulluch 119, 121

I

Imperial Hotel 36, 39, 164
Inghinidhe na hÉireann 46

Irish Citizen Army (ICA)
35, 36, 38, 39, 78, 83,
85, 86, 88, 90, 95, 114,
116, 117, 140, 157,
187, 215
Irish Independent 81, 167,
202
Irish National Aid and
Volunteer Dependants'
Fund (INAVDF) 196,
204, 206
Irish Republican
Brotherhood (IRB) 7,
11, 14, 17, 20, 22, 23,
26, 30, 40, 42, 56, 58,
60, 68, 70, 83, 86, 130,
134, 140, 191, 198,
200, 206
Irish Times, The 80, 81, 83,
101, 104, 142, 163
Irish Transport and
General Workers'
Union (ITGWU) 35,
36, 83, 138
Irish War News 93, 95, 96

J

Jacob's biscuit factory 17,
127, 132, 158, 168
J. W. Elvery & Co. 101,
103

K

Kavanagh, James 154
Keating, Michael 198
Kent, David 182
Kent, Richard 182
Kent, Thomas 179–182
Kent, William 182
Keogh, Gerald 106
Keogh, Michael 62
Kilcoole 51
Kilmainham Gaol 71, 150,
175, 178, 187, 190
Kimmage Garrison 100
King's Own Scottish
Borderers 51

L

Lahiff, Michael 116
Larkfield 97, 98, 100
Larkin, James 35, 36, 39,
85, 138
Lawless, Joseph 130, 133
Lewes Prison 200, 204,
207
Liberty Hall 38, 80, 83,
85, 90, 97, 143, 144,
193
Lomas, Samuel 144, 178
Lonergan, Michael 129
Luce, Arthur 104, 106
Lynch, Diarmuid 40–43
Lynn, Kathleen 187–190,
202

M

MacCurtain, Tomás 179,
180
MacDiarmada, Seán
20–23, 30, 36, 54, 60,
83, 140, 156, 157
MacDonagh, Thomas 16–
19, 85, 127, 175–178
MacNeill, Eoin 40, 42, 43,
48, 52, 68, 73
Mallin, Michael 116–118,
215
Malone, Michael 125, 126
Markievicz, Constance 26,
88, 116, 127
Marrowbone Lane 47,
150, 152, 153
Marshall, Joseph 106
Marsh's Library 158–160
Martyn, Edward 18
Maxwell, General John
173–175, 177, 178
McCabe, Kevin 164
McGallogly, John 100
McGarry, Seán 157
McHugh, Michael 106,
108
Mellows, Liam 134–137
Molloy, Michael 83, 85
Molony, Helena 46, 85

223

Moore Street 144, 154, 156, 157, 187, 196
Mountjoy Prison 190, 200
Mount Street 123, 125, 126
Mulcahy, Richard 130, 132, 194

N

National Volunteers 52, 54, 136
North King Street 150, 170
Northumberland Road 121, 123, 125, 126
Nunan, Ernie 98

O

O'Brien, James 38
O'Brien, William 83, 85
O'Casey, Sean 35, 36
O'Connor, John 'Blimey' 98
O'Donovan Rossa, Jeremiah 56–59, 202
O'Farrell, Elizabeth 157
O'Farrelly, Agnes 44
O'Hanrahan, Michael 168
O'Neill, William 168
O'Rahilly, Michael (The) 149, 154
Ó Riain, Pádraig 129
O'Sullivan, Gearóid 54

P

Pearse, Margaret 72
Pearse, Patrick 15, 17, 24, 26, 36, 56–59, 69–72, 76, 83, 85, 86, 90, 93, 103, 104, 138, 156, 157, 165, 168, 175, 178, 198, 202, 203, 212, 215
Pearse, Willie 69–72
Phoenix Park 80, 161
Plunkett, George 100, 216

Plunkett, Joseph Mary 18, 63, 86, 100, 156, 216
Plunkett, Patrick 157, 196
Portobello Barracks 170
Proclamation of the Irish Republic 7, 8, 15, 77, 83–87, 175, 216

Q

Quinlisk, Timothy 62

R

Redmond, John 33, 46, 52, 54, 55, 59, 171, 173, 200, 210
Redmond, Willie 200
Richmond Barracks 100, 150, 175, 187, 189, 190
Rowe, W. C. 182
Royal College of Surgeons 117, 118, 187
Royal Dublin Fusiliers 30, 119, 121, 126, 153
Royal Irish Constabulary (RIC) 22, 28, 39, 130, 132, 133, 136, 168, 180, 182, 200

S

Sackville (O'Connell) Street 7, 36, 39, 78, 88, 90, 91, 101, 103, 104, 110, 141, 144, 146, 148, 160, 161, 163, 164
Sheehy-Skeffington, Francis 170, 196
Sheehy-Skeffington, Hanna 112
Shelbourne Hotel 114, 116, 118
Sherwood Foresters 125, 126, 144
Sigerson, Dora 212, 214
Sinn Féin 40, 81, 96, 106, 110, 160, 182, 198, 199, 206, 208, 210, 211, 214

Smyth, DI Harry 132
Solemn League and Covenant 31–34
South Dublin Union 95, 150, 152, 214
South Staffordshire Regiment 126, 160
Stanley, Captain H. V. 178
Stanley, Joseph 93
St Enda's 17, 24–30, 69, 70, 71, 97, 98
Stephens, James 82, 148, 167
St Stephen's Green 95, 108, 114, 116–118

T

Tara Street 161
Traynor, Oscar 148, 163
Trinity College, Dublin 104–109, 125, 126, 160, 210

U

Ulster Volunteer Force (UVF) 17, 34, 36, 40, 48, 51
United Irishmen 11, 14, 28

V

Victoria Barracks, Cork 179, 182

W

Whelan, Patrick 136
White, Jack 36
White, Rev. Newport J. D. 160
Wimborne, Viscount 114, 116